TELL THEM SO

A novel

By
Jackie Baters

Cover photo by Kathy Stearns
www.ashotinthepark.biz

author**HOUSE**®

AuthorHouse™
1663 Liberty Drive
Bloomington, IN 47403
www.authorhouse.com
Phone: 1-800-839-8640

Published by AuthorHouse 4/19/2012

ISBN: 978-1-4685-6614-7 (sc)
ISBN: 978-1-4685-6615-4 (e)

This book is dedicated to my husband, Dennis, who said "I do" thirty-eight years ago and still does…

AND

To all those whose lives have been touched by breast cancer….to the survivors and especially to those who have exchanged their pink ribbons for robes of white.

CHAPTER ONE

Darcy SAT ON THE EDGE of her mother's bed saying her final good-bye to the woman she had watched suffer too long. Ironically, it had been eight weeks to the day since the doctor had given Hannah two more months to live. If only the doctor had said four months, or six, or twelve, thought Darcy irrationally. But this was, indeed, Hannah's day of departure, and both women knew it. It was time. What had taken Darcy completely by surprise was the beautiful weather. Somehow she had expected it to be cold and gray the day her mother died, with a chilling wind and raindrops sliding like tears down the windowpane. But there was no wind and there were no raindrops. The sky was a brilliant blue, dotted with cottony white clouds. The cat on the front porch swing was dozing in the warm sunshine. It didn't seem possible to Darcy that death would visit such a lovely setting.

Hannah grasped her only child's hand and sighed. Softly, she spoke, "Well, I didn't make much of an impact on this world, did I sweetheart? When I was a girl I had such wonderful dreams."

It was true that Hannah had dreamed big dreams. From childhood, her only desire had been to serve the Lord, and to serve others in His name. When she had grown up and met Henry Miller, and learned that he shared her dream, she knew they were meant to be. They had married and were thrilled when little Darcy came along. Just as they were finishing their preparations to go to the mission field, Henry had perished in a tragic accident. Hannah, with Darcy still in diapers, had to be practical. Darcy's grandmother happily babysat while Hannah earned her teaching certificate and became an elementary school teacher.

1

"Momma, you raised me and I turned out pretty well." Darcy's voice was barely above a whisper.

"Yes darling, you are, indeed, the one jewel in my crown."

"Now, Momma, don't downplay what you've done for me – been to me – all of my life. I couldn't even remember Daddy as I was so little when he died. All my life it's been you, being both Mother and Father to me – my advisor, teacher, disciplinarian, encourager and life coach- all by yourself. I would never have made it through my teen-age years without you."

"There were times I didn't think either one of us were going to make it," chuckled Hannah.

She can laugh, thought Darcy. She can make a joke and laugh on her deathbed. That's my Momma. No self pity allowed around her!

"Remember, Momma," asked Darcy, "how I was afraid to accept Kyle's marriage proposal and it was you who convinced me that loving him the way I did, it would be fun going through life as Darcy Carsey?'"

"I remember. I was right, wasn't I?"

"Yes, you certainly were. You know how glad I am you talked me into marrying Kyle," Darcy told her.

Hannah smiled weakly." I wanted to do so much more for the needy and hurting people in this world. I've prayed and prayed for forgiveness for not doing more. I've been afraid that God won't be able to say, "*Well done, thou good and faithful servant,*" but I understand- I trust- that because of grace, He'll say '*Good enough.*'"

Even as a saddened Darcy groped for words to comfort and reassure her mother, she heard an odd gasp. She looked into her mother's eyes and saw a sparkling intensity, an almost youthful exuberance. Her mother was seeing something Darcy could not.

Hannah's facial muscles relaxed. The grim look of pain around her mouth was transformed into a smile. She took one deep breath and then no more. Darcy knew her mother was gone, and she knew by the look of intense joy that she had seen on her mother's face in the instant before that last breath that Hannah had died with the peaceful assurance that His grace was indeed sufficient.

Darcy remained beside her mother as several moments silently passed. She smoothed her mother's hair, caressed her stilled hands and finally stood. She bent over the bed and kissed her mother's still warm cheek, one final kiss, and slipped from the room.

Hannah had wanted to die at home and Darcy and Kyle had honored that, even though it had meant moving into Hannah's house these last several weeks. They had slept in Darcy's girlhood bedroom, and Darcy knew that was where Kyle would be now. Earlier he had sat with her by Hannah's bedside, but he had slipped out to give mother and daughter their privacy. When Darcy entered their bedroom, Kyle looked up. His eyes asked the question and hers answered. He rose and wrapped his arms around his wife. Darcy was now an orphan, just as he had been for many years. As Hannah had always been like a second mother to him, he felt like he'd been orphaned all over again.

CHAPTER TWO

HANNAH HAD WISHED TO BE cremated and had made all the pre-arrangements for everything to be taken care of. She died on a Monday and Kyle and Darcy scheduled the memorial service for the following Saturday. That would allow their children, Jared and Claire, to miss as little of their college classes as possible and would be convenient for anyone else who might want to attend. The obituary went into the paper on Tuesday. All across town, people made notes on their calendars.

Letting Jared and Claire know had not been as heart wrenching as Darcy had expected. The young people had half expected the call at any time. Both had hoped to make it home once more to see Hannah, but had made very certain to spend special time with their grandmother the last time they saw her- and to declare their love – just in case they didn't get another opportunity.

Darcy and Kyle had agreed it would be best for him to tell Claire that Grand was gone and she would call Jared. They each loved both of their children fiercely, but Claire had always been Daddy's girl, running into his arms whenever she was hurting. Jared, although having a great relationship with his father, was Darcy's kindred spirit. He always found her a little easier to talk to, a little more able to understand his point of view.

Hannah had been so close to her grandchildren. She simply adored them. When the children were still very young, she had begun pulling each one aside, secretly and individually, and telling him or her that they were her favorite. She knew it wouldn't take them long to share that information. One day, as Kyle was padding along the hallway in sock feet, he heard his children's voices coming from Jared's bedroom. He stopped to listen in, as parents of the very young are permitted to do.

"Grand told me that I was her favorite," said Jared, not yet five years old. Claire, who was three, said "But Grand told me *I* was her favorite!"

Jared responded with big brother patience. "You can't have two favorites, Claire. Favorite means who you like the most."

There was a moment's pause and then Claire piped up in her sweet, happy voice, "Don't you get it, Jared? You're her favorite boy and I'm her favorite girl!"

Kyle chuckled softly and slipped away from his eavesdropping spot. "That Hannah," he thought to himself.

Through the years, Hannah had continued the practice and her grandchildren never tired of it. It became the family's worst kept secret. Everyone knew that everyone else knew that they knew, and yet they all pretended to have not a clue.

Everyone knew, that is, except Darcy. By unspoken agreement, they had all refrained from letting her in the loop, perhaps out of fear she would think it was inappropriate and put an end to their fun.

Jared sensed in his mother's 'hello' the reason for her call. He was determined to make this as easy as possible for her and hold himself together. She informed him of all the particulars and answered his questions. He choked up just a little when he said "She was the most wonderful grandmother a person could ever have."

"You know, Jared," Darcy said slowly and emphatically, "you were her favorite."

Jared roared. He laughed until he couldn't catch his breath. Tears burst from his eyes. When he finally composed himself enough to speak, he said, "Mother, you knew all along, didn't you?! I bet you've known for years."

Darcy answered simply, "I'm not as dumb as you think I am."

Jared laughed again, because he knew that his mother was well aware that he thought she was anything but dumb.

Meanwhile, Kyle was speaking gently to his only daughter. She had responded to the news as he had known she would, questioning and doubting her own behavior. It seemed to be her nature.

"Oh, Daddy, I should have been there. I should have ditched school and been there. I probably talked too much about myself and not enough about her the last time —"

Kyle nipped that in the bud. Cutting her off mid-lament, he said, "Princess, let me tell you something Grand shared with me after your last trip home. She said it was the most beautiful good-bye she could have asked for. She said you were happy and smiling and just delightful. She told me

5

that, if you had come when she was breathing her last breath, you would have been heartbroken, and who would want to see their granddaughter's heart break? She told your mother and me that she hoped that *was* the final good-bye for the two of you because it had been utterly perfect. "

"Did she really say that, Daddy?" implored Claire.

"Yes, honey, she really did," answered Kyle. "You know, Claire, you were her favorite," he added.

"Oh, Daddy, I know I was. She told me!" laughed Claire, and then the laughter turned to sobbing.

CHAPTER THREE

PASTOR PAUL, KYLE AND DARCY prayed together in the pastor's study shortly before Hannah's memorial service was to begin. At ten minutes until 2:00 the men stepped out to tend to a few things giving Darcy a couple of moments to herself. She was thankful for the time alone, to become composed, and allow the Holy Spirit to give her peace.

Out in the sanctuary, Kyle observed with surprise how quickly the pews were filling. He realized they had underestimated what the attendance would be.

Jared and Claire had been milling about visiting with friends they hadn't seen since Christmas break. Even though they had attended this church since infancy they were noticing many unfamiliar faces.

At five until 2:00, the young people found their seats. Kyle slipped into the pastor's study and took Darcy's hand. "It's almost time to begin, Sweetheart," he told her.

"Have many came?" she asked.

"Many more than we expected," replied Kyle. "Are you ready to go in?"

Darcy straightened her shoulders, smoothed the skirt of her blue dress – Hannah had insisted on no black – and smiled. "As ready as I'll ever be" she said. She reached for the pewter urn, beautiful in its simplicity, which held the remains of her beloved mother.

Together, she and Kyle entered the sanctuary as the organist began to play "In the Sweet By and By." Darcy walked to the white clothed table in the front of the church and placed the urn in the very center, between two beautiful vases of pink tulips, Hannah's favorite flowers. She and Kyle moved to the third pew, left side, the exact spot where Hannah had sat and worshipped since before Darcy was born. Their children slid over leaving an aisle seat for Kyle. Darcy sat next to her husband. Claire, to her mother's right, took her hand and held it tightly.

When the organist finished playing, four people in their sixties, two ladies dressed in pink in honor of Hannah's favorite color, and two gentlemen in dark suits, rose from the second pew, right side, and climbed the steps to the platform. A fifth, somewhat younger woman took a seat at the piano.

This group, all friends of Hannah, sang for most of the senior events for the church and was often asked to provide entertainment for other churches and for community events. Not long ago, they had remarked that, as their ages advanced, they would probably start getting requests to do a lot of funerals. To their chagrin, Hannah asked them the very next day if they would plan on singing for her memorial service. It was the first time they had been booked by the deceased, as it were. Of course they said yes. They couldn't imagine anyone else doing the music for their friend Hannah's service.

Hannah had known exactly what she wanted. She had envisioned the entire service in her mind. It would be cheerful – more than cheerful – it would be joyful! It would be a time to remember, but it would also be a time to anticipate. She had not made Darcy promise there wouldn't be any tears, for she knew that was unrealistic. Hannah herself was the emotional sort and would have shed tears at a cat's funeral even if she didn't know the cat. So tears were allowed, but no keening! No dreariness!

Just as Hannah had requested, The King's Quartet broke into a lively rendition of "I'll Fly Away." The way they sang, it was a real toe tapper. Every time Hannah had heard them perform the song, she had thought to herself that it was just what she wanted to have sung when she died.

At the last chorus, the quartet invited the congregation to join in. Their response was so enthusiastic that they repeated the chorus three times before sitting down.

As the music faded, one of the singers stepped forward. He cleared his throat and looked out over the congregation.

"When Hannah first asked us to sing this next song for her she told us it had been a favorite of hers all of her life and that every year it grew sweeter to her. "

He stepped back into place and the pianist began playing the opening refrain of "It Will Be Worth It All When We See Jesus."

Tears flowed down many faces and a number of times 'Amen' and 'Praise the Lord' were heard throughout the room. Darcy squeezed Kyle's hand and smiled at him as they both remembered how often they had heard Hannah humming or singing that song. When the quartet finished, Pastor Paul nodded at Kyle and Kyle went to the podium.

Looking out over the large crowd of faces, both familiar and unfamiliar, Kyle cleared his throat and spoke.

"On behalf of my wife, Darcy, myself, and our children, Jared and Claire, I want to thank you all for honoring the memory of Hannah Miller with your presence. It means so much to us to have you here today.

"Hannah Mast was born on May 2, 1937 to Levi and Sarah Mast. She grew up not twenty miles from this very spot. At the age of twelve, she joined Whispering Springs Community Church. As a child she dreamed of being a missionary and never missed an opportunity to hear a missionary speak or watch a missionary film or read a missionary book. She was supporting missions financially from the time she began receiving an allowance of ten cents a week from her parents.

Hannah Mast met Henry Miller when she was enrolled in college. Their love of Jesus and their passion for missions provided a foundation for a wonderful friendship, which quickly grew into something deeper. They fell in love and set out to follow their dreams together.

On May 22, 1957, Henry and Hannah were married in this very church. Perhaps some of you attended the wedding. Two years later, on October 9, 1959, their only child, Darcy Rose was born and the following week Darcy was dedicated to the Lord right here at this altar.

Henry and Hannah were very close to completing their preparations to go to Africa when Henry was instantly killed in an automobile accident. Hannah had to give up her dreams of the mission field. She received her teacher's certificate and began her career as an elementary school teacher at Whispering Springs Elementary School. She retired after serving there for thirty seven years.

Hannah brought her talent for teaching here to this church as well. She taught the primary girls' Sunday school class so long that some of the charter students are now grandmothers.

She also taught the monthly missionary lessons and was in charge of our missionary reading book program. Additionally she volunteered in our church library.

She was a quiet woman in a way, and yet always cheerful, always ready to listen and encourage.

She was a devoted wife to Henry for the short time they had together. She was a fantastic mother- and father, as well-to Darcy, and a blessing as a mother-in-law. No children ever had a better grandmother than mine, and they will cherish the memories of the times they spent with their Grand. I thank the Lord those times were many.

"I've often heard the phrase 'Our loss is Heaven's gain,' and I can't think of anyone who would exemplify that more than Hannah Miller. She will be missed every day for the rest of our lives, but we thank God that she will never know sorrow or suffering again.

"If any of you would like to share a little something about Hannah this afternoon, or have something you'd like to say, I'd like to give you this opportu…"

Before Kyle could even finish his sentence, a handsome, well dressed man of about forty jumped to his feet and strode purposefully towards the platform. His professional haircut and expensive black suit indicated that he was successful in his field, whoever he was. Neither Kyle nor Darcy recognized him.

The attractive man spoke in a warm, clear voice as he addressed the congregation.

"My name is Jim Baxter," he began, "and I cannot begin to tell you the impact that Hannah Miller had on my life. When I was eleven years old I won the Whispering Springs School spelling bee. I worked hard preparing for the county spelling bee, where I would be representing our school. I was confident I would do well. I even thought I could win. I was humiliated when I came in fifth. I felt like a failure, like I had let everyone down. Mrs. Miller wouldn't have any of that. She told me that fifth out of sixteen was remarkably good for an eleven year old and that I should hold my head up high. She reminded me of some of the hard words I had to spell correctly just to win the local spelling bee. She convinced me that I was a great speller and because of that I fell in love with words-spelling them, reading them, writing them- just fascinated by them. And where do you find more words than anywhere else? In books! I'm a book publisher today, in a profession I enjoy immensely and in which I have enjoyed success. I have Hannah Miller to thank for that – for helping me find the right path in life. I wish I would have come back and told her that, but I never did. She was a wonderful lady.

"I still subscribe to the Whispering Springs paper, and it was there that I read of Mrs. Miller's passing. I just had to come pay my respects."

As Mr. Baxter moved away from the podium, Darcy found herself thinking that she wished Mr. Baxter had been able to let her mother know how well things had turned out for him. It would have pleased her to know her encouragement benefitted him so greatly.

Mr. Baxter was immediately replaced at the podium by a woman in a plain, dark green dress. Darcy and Kyle looked at each other quizzically. This was another person with whom they were unfamiliar. The lady looked a little nervous to be in front of people. Taking a deep breath, she said, "My name is Alice Duncan. I grew up very poor. My father collected eviction notices like some people collect autographs or postage stamps. When I married a good man and finally experienced some financial stability in my life, I became a shopaholic and eventually a hoarder. I'd never had a winter coat before. Now I discovered that if three winter coats made me feel more secure, eight coats made me feel even more so.

"Tom loved me dearly, without a doubt, he did, and I loved him. He tried hard to understand, but it got to where he just couldn't live with the mess. He moved into a small apartment. I felt so terrible. Here he owned a beautiful big house and he was choosing to live alone in a tiny apartment."

She dabbed at her eyes with a tissue and then continued. "One day, I was in a department store buying sheets that were on sale. A pleasant lady in a cheery pink sweater was looking at the sheets, too. I said 'I don't know why I am buying these; I certainly don't need them.' She replied that the sale price was tempting, and she looked right at me. When she did, I saw a look of deep compassion come into her eyes. Suddenly, I realized that she knew. She knew my secret. I didn't know how it could be, but something had told her. She was so kind and gentle. Not a bit judgmental.

She told me about a Christian counselor who had helped a lot of people with all kinds of issues and that I should call her if I ever needed to talk to someone. I'll always remember the way she smiled at me so warmly and said that everybody needs to talk to somebody. She wrote down the counselor's name and number and her own name at the bottom. She told me that she and the counselor had been roommates and good friends in college. 'If you call, tell her Hannah Miller referred you. It will get you an appointment faster.'

"Well, I called that counselor and we started working in earnest on those issues. Things began to take an unbelievable turn for the better. I finally got my house cleared out. I let go of all that stuff – gave it to charity and never missed any of it for a minute. Tom moved back home and we have been as happy as can be ever since. I should have tracked down Mrs.

Miller and told her how much that referral changed my life, but I never did. I wish I had now."

I wish you had too, thought Darcy as Mrs. Duncan took her seat. *I wish Mother could have known how much she touched your life.*

As yet another stranger took over the podium; Darcy shook her head in disbelief. This time, a slim woman in a grey suit and black silk blouse had come forward. "My name is Olivia Turner," she began. "My husband Calvin and I moved to Whispering Springs when we were newlyweds. We were so eager to make friends and be a part of the community, but it wasn't happening. We just weren't connecting with anyone. We were very lonely.

One evening I was at the Laundromat, feeling so blue. The nicest lady was there washing a great big bedspread in the jumbo washer. She said the spread was too big for her washer at home. She was so friendly and sweet that I opened right up to her-a stranger in a Laundromat!

I told her how lonely Cal and I were and I started crying. Hannah Miller comforted me like I was a motherless child. She told me there were several young married couples at her church and invited me to visit. She said you meet a lot of nice people at church.

"I went home and told Cal all about what Mrs. Miller had said. He agreed that it might be a good idea to visit a church, but decided he'd like to try the denomination he grew up in. So we went for a visit and it was amazing how friendly everyone was. They just welcomed us with open arms. Before you knew it, we had lots of friends. But that wasn't the best thing that happened. After we had gone to that church for a little while, Cal rededicated his life to the Lord and then he introduced me to Jesus. We made Christ the head of our home and raised our children in the Christian faith. And it all began with Hannah Miller. She never knew it, because I never did let her know. But I'm glad I was able to be here today, Mr. and Mrs. Carsey, to tell you how much Hannah Miller touched our lives."

Darcy's mind flew back to her mother's words the day she had passed away. She remembered how Hannah had expressed regret for not doing more to help people, for not touching lives the way she should have. If only she had been able to hear these speakers today.

When no else requested to speak, Kyle glanced down at his son, Jared. Jared had asked his dad if it would be all right for him to say something at the service. He wanted so much to honor his grandmother in that way. Kyle had assured his son it would be fine if he was up to it, but that he could change his mind if he wanted to when the time came.

As father and son connected visually, Jared gave a slight nod. He stood and slowly came forward. The nearer he got to the front of the church, the more purposeful and determined his steps became. Darcy, observing her son, thought to herself that she could sense the Lord giving him courage.

Jared took his place behind the podium. He looked at his parents and his sister and they smiled their encouragement.

"If you think you have or had the world's greatest grandmother, I'm sorry to inform you that you would be wrong. That would be my grandmother. She was second to none. Grand taught me my numbers, letters and colors when I was a toddler. When I entered kindergarten everyone thought I was a genius because I was so far ahead of the rest of the class. I'm not a genius, believe me. The only thing special about me was that I had a special grandmother. Grand was real big on teachable moments. If I was about to do something wrong or dangerous or stupid she didn't yell 'stop.' She hugged me and explained why I shouldn't do it. If she were in the garden, she didn't just let me play in the dirt beside her. She showed me what she was doing and let me help. Same way in the kitchen.

I guess Grand's best and most significant teaching moments had to do with Jesus. She never missed a chance to tell me about God the Father and Jesus, His Son. She was a walking Sunday School, but she always made it interesting and fun.

When Grand was diagnosed with cancer, I thought my world was caving in, but she straightened me out quick. She told me all about how wonderful her life had been and about all the ways the Lord had blessed her. She said that as much as she loved being here with me and Claire and Mom and Dad, that being in Heaven would be more wonderful than anyone could ever imagine. She said that when her time came to die she wouldn't be one bit afraid and I shouldn't be either. She told me that maybe she'd survive the cancer- that lots of people do. But she said that for the believer, it was a win/win situation. If she lived – yahoo. But if she died, she'd go to Heaven – Hallelujah!"

There was a ripple of soft laughter and several people said, "Amen" in response to that. Jared laughed himself and then said, "So, since Grand did die, I guess it would be appropriate for all of us together to say 'Hallelujah!'" He raised his arms as if directing a choir and led the congregation in shouting "Hallelujah!"

With that, Jared returned to his seat and Kyle stood again behind the podium. He said "It has warmed the hearts of my family to hear such wonderful stories of the impact our Hannah has had on the lives of you who have spoken here today. To each of you and to everyone here, we express our appreciation for honoring the memory of Hannah Mast Miller with your presence. God bless you all."

With a slight nod to the King's Quartet, Kyle left the platform and took his seat beside Darcy. The singers reassembled themselves and prepared to do their final number.

It was a contemporary song and one they had never sung publically before. Recorded by the gospel group, "Mercy Me," it was titled "I Can Only Imagine." They were nervous about performing it, but had included much prayer with their intense rehearsal, and were trusting the Lord to help them. As they began to sing, a peace and joy that passes understanding flowed from heaven, through them and across the sanctuary. As one, the congregation rose to their feet and sang along here and there whenever they knew the words.

When the song ended, Pastor Paul stepped forward and asked everyone to remain standing for prayer. The minister had intended to speak, but decided not to deliver his entire message. After a beautiful, heartfelt prayer, he addressed the people.

"Friends," he said, "Nothing I could say today would do any more to honor Hannah than the words already spoken by all of you. I do, however, have a very important message for you from Hannah herself. She wrote these words and asked me – no, implored me – to read them at her service. Hear my friends, the words of Hannah Mast Miller.

"If you haven't accepted Jesus as your Savior, come to Him today. He will be your Friend and your Guide, your Rock and your fortress. He will be your strength in times of weakness and your comforter in times of sorrow. He will give you joy unspeakable and full of glory. Life is short; eternity is long. Seek Him while you still can. It's the best way to live and the only way to die."

"The best advice you will ever receive, dear ones, brought to you today by Hannah Miller. I would be happy to meet in my study with anyone who would like to pray with me there. Meanwhile the ladies have prepared a beautiful meal and we invite you, one and all, to join us in the fellowship hall. Thank you so much."

As the pastor stepped down from the platform, Kyle and his family slipped out of their pew. They made their way down the aisle to the foyer and formed a line just inside the front door. As people filed by, the family accepted the many hugs, kisses, handshakes and warm words of sympathy offered them.

"What a beautiful service," so many said. "We will miss her so much," was often heard. The family thanked each one and asked them to please stay and eat. Most said they would, especially those who were members of Whispering Springs Community Church, and others who were close friends and neighbors. Somehow Jim Baxter, the book publisher, had slipped past them and they didn't get a chance to speak with him. The ex-hoarder, however, was a chatty, friendly sort of person and said she's be delighted to stay if it was all right.

That night an exhausted Darcy stretched out on the sofa with her feet in Kyle's lap. The foot rub he was giving her made her sigh with pleasure. It felt so good to be home at last, relaxing in her comfortable blue and white pajamas and blue bathrobe. It had been a long day.

"Honey," Kyle asked, "Were you pleased with the service?"

Darcy nodded. "It was so much better than I envisioned it would be. In fact, I'm sure it was much better than even Mom ever dreamed it would be." She pointed her finger at her husband, "You, sir, did a wonderful job," she told him. "And Jared's tribute was just beautiful. I can't get over how many people were there, especially people you and I didn't know. I'm sure Mom wasn't expecting a packed house.

"Kyle, with everything happening this week, I really hadn't had the time to talk to you about my last conversation with my mother. She said something so sad." Darcy paused and Kyle waited silently for her to continue. Darcy sat up. She leaned her head on Kyle's shoulder and continued, "She said she hadn't done as much as she'd hoped with her life, that she hadn't touched as many people as she should have, that she hadn't affected the lives of hurting, needy people, and that she hadn't made the impact for the Lord that she wished she had."

"She should have come to her own memorial service!" exclaimed Kyle.

"I know!" said Darcy. "I keep thinking about all the things those people said and about how she didn't know about any of it. She had no idea! I know she didn't do any of it for credit or recognition and she would have given God all the glory, anyway- but it would have been such an encouragement to her if they had just told her while she was alive how much her actions had affected their lives. If she'd only known how much they appreciated her, she might not have felt the way she did when she died.

"Kyle, if we care about someone, if we appreciate someone and are grateful for something they've done, we should tell them so. We should, Kyle. We should tell them while they are still alive," said Darcy.

Kyle stretched, worked the kinks out of his neck and patted Darcy's leg, "You are absolutely right, honey. We SHOULD tell them so. And right now I want to tell you how much I appreciate the sweet spirit you've had this week in the midst of your sorrow and how thankful I have been for the way your strength has made it so much easier for the rest of us."

"Prayer," answered Darcy. "Prayer makes all the difference. How do people make it through the hard places without prayer, Kyle?"

"Sometimes they don't, honey. That's why we always need to keep praying that they will find the Lord someday," said Kyle.

"We certainly do," agreed Darcy. "and right now, Kyle, I think it is time for me to say my prayers and go to bed. I'm exhausted. The kids already turned in. What time are we leaving to take them back to school tomorrow?"

"Right after church," answered Kyle. "We'll grab a bite on the road."

"Okay. Good night, sweetheart," said Darcy. "Good night, honey, sleep well." Kyle told her.

"For the first night this week, I believe I will," she replied.

CHAPTER FOUR

IN THE WEEKS FOLLOWING HANNAH'S memorial service, Darcy and Kyle received phone calls, sometimes as many as three or four, every single day. Some were from people who had attended Whispering Springs Community Church long ago. When they heard from old friends that Hannah had passed, they called to pay their respects and to share their stories of the ways in which Hannah had touched their lives.

There were calls from people with whom Hannah had taught school, and they too, had stories to tell. Not a few of the calls were from former students of Hannah's, both elementary school and Sunday school.

One afternoon Hannah was playing a CD and almost didn't hear the phone in time to catch the call. "Hello", she said into the phone a little breathlessly.

"Oh, I've called at a bad time," said an unfamiliar feminine voice.

"Not at all," replied Darcy. "How can I help you?"

"Darcy? It's Arlene Matthews."

"Mrs. Matthews! I haven't spoken to you in ages-not since you and Mr. Matthews retired and moved to Florida. Mother mentioned you not four months ago. She said nobody could make a better lemon meringue pie than Arlene Matthews."

"Actually, I was calling about your mother, Darcy. I heard from my sister that she had passed away."

"Yes," answered Darcy. "She had cancer and it took her quite quickly."

"She was such a lovely woman, Darcy. You were blessed to have her for a mother."

"I certainly was," Darcy agreed.

"Darcy, you don't know this. You were just a little girl. But when I was

17

young and Kenneth and I were trying to start a family, I miscarried three times in a row," the older woman confided.

"Oh, Mrs. Matthews, I'm so sorry to hear that! How awful for you," Darcy murmured compassionately.

"It *WAS* awful," Arlene Matthews replied. "I couldn't understand it. I was so unhappy. It just didn't make sense to me that everyone around me was having babies but I was being denied that joy. It seemed to me that some of the couples we knew who were becoming parents were much less qualified for the job than we were. I remember going to a baby shower and coming home to tell Kenneth that the girl having the baby didn't have the sense God had given a goose and *SHE* was going to get to be a mother.

"I begged God for a baby- begged and pleaded and cried. Great big fat tears of self pity. One day your mother and I got to talking about babies. I told her about how my miscarriages were affecting me emotionally and spiritually, how I felt so sorry for myself, and to be honest, a little confused about God.

"Darcy, your mother knew all the right things to say to me. She didn't judge me. She didn't scold me. She didn't tell me to just get over it, the way some people would. She let me talk it out. She allowed me to confess the fears I'd been hiding-that maybe God thought I wouldn't be a good mother. Maybe He thought a baby deserved someone better than me. She did a lot of listening, because I had a lot to say. Then she told me straight out that God wants to be first in our lives, that He needs to be Number One, and that He wants us to accept His will for our lives. She said He doesn't expect us to always understand it, or maybe even be able to make any sense of it, but, nevertheless, to accept it. Then she prayed for me. She prayed those very words over me. After that, I started praying, myself, that I would come to a place of accepting God's will for my life, even if it meant I'd never be a momma. I didn't think it was possible, but I finally did reach that point. I truly did find myself saying "Lord, if I never have a child I will still love you and serve you and be happy with the life you have given me. And I meant it, too!"

When Arlene Matthews finally stopped to take a breath, Darcy spoke up. "Mrs. Matthews, I know for a fact that you were the only woman to ever give birth to triplets in this part of the state!"

"Yes, Darcy," laughed Arlene merrily. That is the honest truth. When I finally surrendered the whole situation to God, when I decided I wasn't going to let my joy in life be determined by me getting what I want ,when I want it, I had honestly thought I would go through life childless. And I was ok with that. Three months later I was pregnant!"

Mrs. Matthews was on a roll. She continued, saying, "Your mother helped me so much with that, too, Darcy. The devil tried to use those miscarriages to put fear in my heart, but your mother kept reminding me that God is not the author of fear. She told me to stand on the scripture, CASTING ALL YOUR CARE UPON HIM, FOR HE CARES FOR YOU. And boy did I! Turned out the pregnancy went just fine. When the triplets came, healthy as could be, I finally realized something. Those babies coming into the world was more about them than it was about me. God had a special plan for their lives and a special time frame in which they were to fulfill those plans. What right did I have to ask God to throw the whole universe out of sync' by having someone born before God wanted them to be born? If I had just grasped that earlier I could have saved myself so much angst, so much drama, and so much misery. I could have been so much happier."

"Anyway, Darcy," concluded Mrs. Matthews, when she was about talked out, "I didn't mean to take so much of your time. But I just had to share with you how much your mother's kindness and prayers and wise counsel meant to me at such a difficult time in my life."

"Mrs. Matthews, your call has meant so much to me," Darcy assured her. But before you go, if you don't mind my asking, what was it like raising triplets?"

"Oh, my dear," gushed Mrs. Matthews. "It was wonderful. It was like God had given us a baby in place of each one we had lost. Like Job, you know! It was so exciting. But, of course, then we had to go home from the hospital. Sometimes I was literally tempted to question God all over again in reverse-as in why in the world would He give someone as inadequate as me three children to raise! I finally decided God had a great sense of humor and I was going to need one, too. So, with His help, I developed one. Ask my kids. Our house was always full of laughter. And after all these years Kenneth and I still make each other laugh."

"Ok now," Arlene said firmly. "I absolutely have to go now. You take care, Darcy. And listen, honey, don't let anyone try to tell you the right way to grieve or how long you are allowed to grieve. You do what is best for YOU."

"Thank you, Mrs. Matthews, I'll do that. And thank you so much for calling."

When Darcy hung up, she stood there a few moments reflecting on what her mother's friend had shared. A large smile suddenly lit up Darcy's face. She had just realized that Mrs. Matthews had made her laugh. It was the first time she'd laughed since her mother died.

for the one who received this Bible that they would come to know Jesus as their Savior. I'd never had anyone to pray for me before that I knew of and just thinking about it brought tears to my eyes. And believe me, I wasn't one to do much crying in those days.

One other thing I found in that Bible was one of those gospel tracts. I read it and it explained all about how everyone had sinned and all of those sins had been recorded in a book. Some people had really long lists and some people had lists that maybe weren't as long as others, but everybody had a list-no exceptions. Now people try all kinds of ways to keep their list a secret or to make it go away. Maybe they just deny that it exists or lie about what is on it. Maybe they try to have a list of good deeds that is longer than their list of sins. Maybe they give a whole bunch of money to a church or some charity or something. But none of those things erases the list. In fact there is not one single thing anybody can do to get rid of that list. Now here is the exciting part. The tract said that Jesus took our sins upon Himself when he went to the cross. It said He already paid the penalty for our sins. If you accept Him as your savior, He signs His name over yours at the bottom of the list and his signature is written with His own blood.

That tract said we are all sinners and we can be set free from our sins by the blood of Jesus. Well, being set free sounds mighty nice to someone who is literally in prison. I thought about that tract a lot. I couldn't stop thinking about why Jesus would do that, and I couldn't get that part about the blood out of my mind.

Once I started reading the Bible, I couldn't quit. I went through the Old Testament pretty quick until I got bogged down in the Chronicles. So I thought I'd go over to the New Testament for awhile. When I read in the Gospels all about Jesus it just clicked in my mind about Him being the Passover Lamb. I had really liked that part in the Old Testament. I guess I could kind of identify with people in bondage. So I started connecting everything together and coming to an understanding of the blood of Jesus. One night I got that tract out and read it again. Then I got down on my knees and laid my Bible on the cot in front of me.

"Lord," I prayed, "My sins are many and you know them all. I guess if this tract was about me the list would have to be three times as long as anyone's. But I'm seeing in your word that forgiveness is for whoever will ask for it, no matter how long their list of sins is or how bad they've been. So I'm asking you, Lord, please forgive my sins. Please save me. I guess I won't be able to do much for you being here in prison, but I will live for you and follow you and do the very best I can. Please come into my heart."

Well, let me tell you. There was no reason to wonder if He heard me. This feeling, this sensation came over me. It was like a pitcher of liquid joy had been poured right over my head and it was running all down over my body, seeping into every pore. If I would have gotten a pardon from the governor and then won the lottery the same day, it couldn't have made me half so happy.

I have led seventy-five inmates to the Lord since then. Many of them have been released and I pray for them every day that they will stay true to the Lord and not end up back in here. There have been a few guys who came in here just like I did, tough as nails and reeking with attitude, but it's funny how praying for someone, just caring for them, can sometimes make that attitude melt like butter. It worked for me. Hannah Miller cared enough to give me that brand new Bible and she prayed for me. She didn't know my story; she didn't even know my name, but she prayed for me. It's like the Bible says about planting and watering and God giving the increase. Hannah planted, and seventy-six men who were once hard cases are now serving the Lord. I hope it will be a lot more than that before it's over. I've still got plenty of time to do my in-house prison ministry. I'm in here for life. I was convicted of murder.

Anyway, that's my story. Remember me in your prayers and I will remember you.

> Your friend in Christ,
> Leonard Brown

Kyle laid down the letter and looked at Darcy. Tears glittered in her eyes. She was unable to speak, but Kyle managed to say "Wow", huskily.

Momentarily, Darcy said in a quivering voice, "I had no idea, no idea at all."

"Neither did I," responded Kyle, "but I'm glad he wrote. Won't Jared and Claire be thrilled?"

"You know, honey," Darcy said, "I've been thinking. Ever since Mom died we have been hearing so many stories about how she touched the lives of people. There were the ones at the memorial service and loads of others. I've lost track of the phone calls. This letter and the two cards you brought in today make 117 pieces of correspondence. 117! I just counted yesterday out of curiosity. Do you realize that the common thread running through all of these stories is that none of these people ever really communicated to Mom the impact she had on their lives? I've got this idea percolating in the back of my mind that maybe I should pull all the stories together into a little book for Jared and Claire. I think I'd kind of emphasize the thought that if you're thankful for something someone has done for you, or if someone has been a blessing to you, you should tell them so. Make it a life lesson for the kids. One of those teachable moments for which Jared said Mom was famous. What do you think?"

Kyle smiled lovingly at his wife. "Sweetie, I think it is a terrific idea. I not only think you should do it, I'm going to keep after you until you do!"

"All right , then," said Darcy. She squared her shoulders and got that WOMAN ON A MISSION look that Kyle knew so well. He realized then that she would be consumed with the project now that she had made up her mind.

CHAPTER SIX

EVERY SPARE MINUTE DARCY COULD find was dedicated to her writing project. There were many tears shed as she put down on paper the stories she had recently been told about her mother. She realized she was grieving in a very healthy way. She'd even come to terms with the realization that her mother had died not knowing how much she had touched the lives of others, nor the impact she had made in her quiet, caring way. Gently, and yet firmly, Darcy had felt the Lord urging her to let go of her pain. She couldn't do anything about the past, but maybe she could use the omissions of the past to help her children, and Kyle and herself as well, be more aware of the need to verbalize their appreciation to others and to let them know what a blessing they had been.

TELL THEM SO. TELL THEM SO. Those three words kept resonating in Darcy's head. She decided that the title of the little project she was doing for Jared and Claire would have to be just that-*TELL THEM SO.*

The kids would not be home for the summer. They both had jobs as counselors at a wonderful Christian camp. It was hard to believe that Jared would be a junior and Claire a sophomore when they returned to college in the fall. Jared's chosen field of meteorology was very demanding and he had a long road ahead of him. Claire had felt called to the nursing profession, which both Kyle and Darcy agreed suited her perfectly.

With her children gone, Darcy was able to work long and openly on her project, which she had decided would be a surprise.

While running errands one day, Darcy was detained at a railroad crossing. As a remarkably long train slid past her, she began to think about her Aunt Sally. She had taken a train ride with Aunt Sally, her father's sister, once when she was a very young girl. Darcy had been too little when her father

died to remember anything, but she knew from things that Hannah had said that Aunt Sally had been a huge help through that dark and difficult time. Hannah had been amazed that Sally, who was so grief stricken over the loss of her only sibling, could be so attentive to the needs of Hannah and her child. For a solid year, Sally took charge of every holiday, welcoming Hannah and Darcy into her home and making their first Thanksgiving and Christmas and Easter without Henry pleasant experiences. She even made Valentine's Day and the 4th of July festive.

Darcy suspected that Sally had been a big help financially as well. Once when Hannah was showing Darcy some old family photographs, Darcy had commented several times that she had certainly been a well dressed little girl. "Oh, your Aunt Sally just loved shopping for you and dressing you up," Hannah had responded. "She had all boys, you know."

Aunt Sally had not been able to make it to Hannah's memorial service. Uncle Bill had Alzheimer's and Sally rarely left his side. She had sent a beautiful card and the sweetest letter, though.

Darcy decided that the minute she got home she needed to call Aunt Sally. "Hurry up, train," she muttered as she waited for the end of the train to appear. The moment the guard rail lifted, Darcy was over the tracks and zipping down the road.

After taking the old photo album off the shelf and settling into an easy chair, Darcy placed the call to her aunt. She let the phone ring several times as she knew how often Sally was busy tending to her husband.

"Hello!" Aunt Sally's voice was a little breathless, but cheerful, when she finally answered on the fourteenth ring.

"Aunt Sally, hi! It's Darcy."

"Oh, Darcy; oh, honey. I'm so glad you didn't give up on me answering the phone. Uncle Bill, you know."

"I know," answered Darcy. "It's so good to hear your voice."

"So, honey, how are you, really? Are you getting along ok?" asked Sally, with genuine concern.

"You know, Aunt Sally, I really am," Darcy assured her. "It does get easier with time. I miss Mom and I always will, but every day gets a little easier."

"Well, you and your mother were always so close. It was just the two of you for so long," said Sally.

"I'm not sure that's really so, Aunt Sally," Darcy replied quickly, "I don't know that it was just the two of us. If it had been, I don't know if we'd have made it. I've been thinking about how much you were there for

Mom and me when Daddy died. I know Mom leaned on you a lot and you didn't allow me to be without anything I needed. I have no doubt that Mom expressed her appreciation to you, but it has occurred to me that I never have."

"My dear girl! Your mother thanked me for both of you so constantly that I had to command her to stop. I don't think your mother ever realized how much doing for my brother's only child comforted me and helped me deal with losing him."

"Well, Aunt Sally, I just want you to know what a blessing you have been to me. Thank you for all you've done over the years and just thank you for being you."

Sally was on the verge of tears as she replied, "Sweetheart, you have no idea how much this call has meant to me." Just then, Darcy heard some kind of loud noise in the background and wondered what it could be.

"Oh my, honey. I have to run! Uncle Bill, you know. Sorry to cut this short," said Aunt Sally in a rush.

"You go," said Darcy. "Love you."

"Love you, too!" With that the call was ended.

Before the day was over, Darcy had called three more people. She was pleased to think that she was actually becoming the first student to learn the *Tell Them So* lesson she had hoped to teach her children. 'Makes sense,' she thought to herself. 'You can't teach what you don't know.'
Darcy continued to work on her writing project almost every day. The problem, if you could call it a problem, was that she couldn't decide which stories to leave out. The project was getting much longer than she had originally anticipated. But, truly, which stories could she not include? Each of them had been such a blessing to her. She began to realize that she wouldn't be finished until almost Christmas. This would be Jared and Claire's Christmas present this year, this and the traditional new pairs of pajamas. The pajama thing was getting to be a challenge now that young people slept in such strange things.

Darcy decided she needed to finish the writing portion of her project by mid-November. That would give her time to put together a nice Thanksgiving for her family. Then, when the kids went back to school, she would have time to tweak it and to make the covers she had already designed in her head. She'd selected a picture of Grand, Jared and Claire, taken when Jared was seven and Claire, five. That meant that the deadline for material to be included was now- right now- today. She was still getting an occasional call from someone who had been a student in Hannah's class Sunday school class, or an old friend or colleague. . Someone would hear from someone else, who had heard from yet another party, that Hannah had passed away, and Darcy would receive another call or letter from someone paying their respects and perhaps sharing yet another story. That was very nice, but nothing anybody had yet to say would be able to interfere with Darcy's deadline.

Darcy's shoulder was to the wheel, her nose to the grindstone, her pen to the page. Willpower, perseverance and fast food take out would guarantee her success. She didn't watch television, she didn't go to her book club meeting and she eventually almost cancelled her weekly Friday night date with Kyle-but he vetoed that idea.

"Honey, I'll help you make up the time if there's any way I can, but you need to get out of the house and I kind of need your undivided attention," Kyle told her.

So Kyle and Darcy kept their tradition of date night. On their first night out together after Kyle had insisted that their routine not be changed, Darcy was determined not to mention her project. Kyle seemed to like that, so the topic of conversation became the impending Thanksgiving holiday. Darcy mentioned how eager she was for the kids to be home. Kyle's comments seemed to all center around the food they would be having for Thanksgiving dinner.

"It will be all the usual things," promised Darcy. "Turkey, dressing, mashed potatoes and gravy, cranberries, green bean casserole, squash, apple pie, mince meat pie and pumpkin pie."

"Ah, pumpkin pie," sighed Kyle, a look of bliss on his smiling face. "I can hardly wait. You know, honey, three pies for four people is a bit much. You shouldn't go to so much bother."

"And whose favorite would you have me omit?" asked Darcy. "Claire's apple pie or Jared's mince meat pie? I guess I could forget about the pumpkin pie since I can make you one any old time."

"What?!" shouted Kyle. Then, lowering his voice a few decibels as he remembered he was in public, he looked pleadingly into Darcy's eyes and said "No pumpkin pie on Thanksgiving Day? Sacrilege! I won't hear of it."

Darcy laughed. "Ok, then. Three pies it is!"

As she slipped under the covers that night, Darcy reflected contentedly on what a pleasant evening she and Kyle had just shared. Kyle had been so right about her needing to get out of the house. But in the morning, she told herself sternly, it was back to work

CHAPTER SEVEN

On the Friday before Thanksgiving, Darcy sat alone at her desk and shouted, "Praise the Lord!" She had finished the writing phase of her project. A feeling of deep satisfaction settled over her. She was already envisioning giving the kids this unique and special gift. She pushed her chair away from the desk, stood up and stretched. Now to focus on Thanksgiving, she thought to herself.

Darcy pulled on her black wool coat and gathered up her purse and gloves. She needed to get to the grocery store while there were still turkeys and cans of cranberry sauce to be had.

As Darcy pointed her heavily laden cartful of groceries toward the checkout lane, she thought about how thankful she was that she had been able to get to the supermarket on Friday rather than Saturday. Even though the store was busy, Darcy had been able to find a convenient parking space, and the store had not been sold out of a thing on her list. She knew that the next day, the Saturday before Thanksgiving, it would be much more crowded.

Passing a freezer compartment featuring whipped topping on sale, Darcy realized that she had not put that on her grocery list. How in the world could she have forgotten that, she wondered. Kyle always had whipped topping on his pumpkin pie. Always! She was just reaching into the freezer for two tubs of topping when a voice behind her called out, "Darcy? Darcy Carsey? Is that you?" Darcy turned and faced old Mrs. Lawson, who had served as the Whispering Springs librarian for thirty six years.

"Why, Mrs. Lawson, it's wonderful to see you! Didn't you move to Arizona after you retired?" asked Darcy.

"Yes, I sure did. I love it out there. My kids flew me home for Thanksgiving. I suspect they had a motive. They had me here for Thanksgiving and they will expect me to have them in Arizona for Christmas. Fine with me! What matters is being together as a family." She colored a bit then, as if embarrassed to have misspoken.

"Oh Darcy," said Mrs. Lawson, "I'm so sorry about your mother. I didn't know she had passed until I got back in town. She was such a sweet, sweet woman, Darcy, and so generous."

"She was indeed a sweet lady, Mrs. Lawson," agreed Darcy.

"And don't forget generous. Every single month for all those years she taught school she donated a good, clean parent-approved book to the juvenile section of our town library. She said she wanted our young people to have something uplifting to read," Mrs. Lawson told her.

"I didn't know that," said Darcy.

"Oh, my dear, it was so frustrating! People were forever telling me how much they appreciated what fine books their children were finding at the library and thanking me for stocking them. I couldn't give credit where it was due because your mother insisted on being an anonymous donor. But I figured that since she's gone and all it was ok to say something. It was ok, wasn't it?" Mrs. Lawson asked, coloring again.

"Why, yes, Mrs. Lawson. It certainly was. I'm glad you told me," responded Darcy.

Mrs. Lawson smiled. "Well, I'd better scoot. Happy Thanksgiving to you and yours," she called over her shoulder as she pushed her cart away.

As Darcy reflected on what Mrs. Lawson had said, she thought back on how much she and her mother had enjoyed talking about books. Hannah's goal of instilling in Darcy a life-long love and appreciation for the written word had certainly been achieved. Darcy had always realized that Hannah was steering her towards books that were inspiring to young people. She never guessed that Hannah was recommending books that Hannah, herself, had made sure were on the library shelves. How like her mother to donate the books to the library so that not only Darcy, but the whole community would have access to them, rather than giving them exclusively to her daughter.

As Darcy was loading her groceries into her car, she thought about her writing project. It was too bad she hadn't run into Mrs. Lawson earlier. Spilling the beans, as she had, about the anonymous donations to the library would have made a great addition to her book. But a deadline is a deadline, she told herself firmly.

One more errand and Darcy could go home and get busy with holiday preparations. Findley's apple orchard, on the outskirts of Whispering Springs, had the best apple cider to be found anywhere. Darcy always stocked up on it at this time of year.

Darcy smiled as she pulled up in front of the small scale, barn-like structure painted a cheery red and white. As she stepped along the walkway, she admired the tasteful fall décor. It was such a pleasant scene, with a wheelbarrow full of bright orange pumpkins, pots of chrysanthemums, and an antique cider press with baskets of apples leaning against it. Darcy pushed open the front door and was happy to see that Mary Anne Findley was working the counter. The two women had been friends for years, although they were often both too busy to see much of each other. Mary Anne was with another customer, so Darcy wandered the aisles selecting items to purchase. Into her cart went two baskets of red delicious apples, four gallons of cider and some cinnamon scented candles. A green apron with red apples on it, with a matching pair of potholders, made her smile, so she dropped them in also.

Mary Anne was alone when Darcy approached the counter. As Darcy unloaded her cart, she laughed. "I always buy more than I mean to when I come in here and I never regret it," she said.

"I'm so glad to see you, Darcy," said Mary Anne. "Any chance you have a minute to talk?"

"I've got groceries out in the car, but sure, Mary Anne, I've got a few minutes. What's up?"

"Well, where should I begin? You know I'm adopted, right?"

" Why, yes, of course, Mary Anne. Your folks never kept it a secret from you or anyone else. What about it?"

Mary Anne smiled. "Awhile back I became curious about my birthmother. I told my mom that I wouldn't pursue the idea of trying to find the woman if it would hurt Mom or upset her even the slightest bit. She said that it was only natural that I would be curious about my birthmother, since I'd always known she was out there somewhere. So with my Mom's blessing I did a search. To tell you the truth, I didn't really believe I'd really track her down. I didn't intend to go to the ends of the earth or anything. Turns out it was a whole lot easier than I thought it was going to be-and I found her!"

"Oh, Mary Anne, that's wonderful!" exclaimed Darcy. "Um, I mean, is it? Have you met her? Did it go well?" she asked.

"I did meet her and it went very well, thank you. Come to find out, she was from around here. I guess that's part of what made the search so easy. But Darcy, here's the big thing. She confessed to me that she almost aborted me!"

"What!?" shrieked Darcy, as she grabbed the counter to steady herself.

"Yes! She explained to me that she was desperate and ashamed and she was all ready to go through with it."

"What stopped her?" Darcy asked softly.

"Your mother did." Mary Anne looked at her friend and smiled broadly.

"My mother did," said Darcy. It wasn't so much a question as an acknowledgement of information received. "My mother stopped your mother from aborting you," said Darcy in a dazed tone, and then repeated herself. "My mother stopped your mother from aborting you."

"That's what my birthmother told me. She said she hadn't breathed a word to anyone about being pregnant. Her own parents didn't even know. But somehow your mother figured it out. She asked my mother to go for a walk with her and your mother was so sweet. She told my birthmother that everyone makes mistakes, but sometimes when they try to fix it they make an even bigger mistake. She said that two wrongs don't make a right-they just make things worse. Hannah told my birthmother that she would regret it to her dying day if she ended my precious life. She said God loved every unborn child and that my life was not hers to take.

"Darcy, your mom prayed with my birthmother and my mother turned everything over to the Lord. She decided to put me up for adoption. She went away to have me, but not very far, and the Findley's contacted the very adoption agency handling my birthmother's case. Do you realize what I am telling you? Your mother saved my life-before I was even born! There wouldn't even be a Mary Anne Findley if it wasn't for her. I've been kind of thinking of her as yet another mother to me because she had so much to do with me coming into the world." It was such a thrill for Mary Anne to be able to share this news with her friend.

Darcy tried to speak, and then just stood there smiling and staring at Mary Anne. When she finally found her voice, she said "Honey, I've been hearing some pretty amazing stories about my mother ever since she died, but this is the best one of all."

"It is amazing, isn't it!" declared Mary Anne "I wanted to go to your mom and tell what I had learned and thank her, but by the time I found all this out she was so sick, and then she died before I got there. Darcy, how could I have failed to get there in time to tell her how much what she did meant to me-and to my family?" Mary Anne's chin quivered as a single tear slid down her cheek. "I've been so upset with myself that I couldn't even tell you about it until now."

Darcy hesitated just for a moment and then smiled as she spoke to her friend in a tone rich with compassion and kindness. "The past is past, honey. We don't always get another chance to do the things we've left undone. But the future is still before you. From here on out, if there is anyone who has been a blessing to you, be sure to tell them so. Tell them while you still can."

I've learned my lesson, Darcy Carsey, and I thank you for the admonition! I will never forget this conversation," promised Mary Anne.

The two women gathered up Darcy's purchases and carried them out to the car. Just as they were saying goodbye to each other, Darcy touched her friend's arm. "Mary Anne, I've been putting together some stories about the impact my mother's life had on various people into a little book for my children. Your story belongs in there as much as, and maybe even more than, any of the others I've gathered up. If I am very careful to keep it anonymous, could I have your permission to include it?" asked Darcy.

"Oh, my goodness!" cried Mary Anne. "Please, please do. It would make me feel so much better about never thanking Hannah. And don't worry about the anonymous part. My birth mother has decided not to be in hiding anymore. When she met me, she told me that if she'd known her secret was so beautiful she would never have been able to keep me a secret at all," she said, and blushed a deep crimson. "She's coming for Thanksgiving. Wasn't it great of Mom and Dad to invite her?"

Darcy agreed that happy endings-or maybe in this case she should say happy beginnings- were always wonderful. She hugged her friend tightly and then said that she had to get home with her groceries.

Back at the house, Darcy hurried to put away all the food she had purchased, tending to the perishables first. Thank goodness they were all in insulated bags. Those had been her mother's idea. Darcy used them because her mother had. Oh, Mom, she thought, how many things do I do because that's the way you taught me? In how many ways, great and small, did you influence and shape my life? No one can say I'm just like you, because you were sweeter, kinder and more patient than I'll ever be, but your handprint is all over my life.

Darcy leaned against the counter and began to cry. Well, how stupid was this? She thought she was done with all this crying, and here she was blindsided by some silly, insulated shopping bags. Good grief! But even as she chided herself, Darcy realized that it was more than that. The groceries and the insulated bags represented Thanksgiving dinner and this would be her first one without her mother. Darcy pulled herself together. Enough of this! She was anxious to get back to her writing project. So much for thinking it was done. She quickly stowed the rest of the groceries and then returned to her desk. Had it been just this morning that she had been so pleased to be finished? Well, she wasn't finished after all-not quite yet. She'd known that as soon as she'd heard Mary Anne's awesome story.

This shouldn't be too hard, she thought. She just needed to add Mary Anne's story and then move the end of the book to follow that. She might as well include Mrs. Lawson's story, too, while she was at it. She could do this. After that, the book would be truly finished, she promised herself.

It didn't take that long, really. Darcy began with Mrs. Lawson's rather short story and then moved on to Mary Anne's. The words just flowed onto the page as she recounted the wonderful things she had heard that day. It was such a beautiful way to end the book. She didn't mind the extra work at all.

Finishing up-for the last time-Darcy decided to fix a genuine home cooked meal for her long suffering husband. No leftover pizza heated in the microwave tonight. She bustled about, humming to herself, and enjoying the anticipation of seeing Kyle's face when he came through the door. Her timing was perfect. The roast chicken was ready to put on the table just as Kyle walked into the house.

"Wow," Kyle said. "Something smells wonderful." He strode straight to his wife and took her in his arms. "Oh, it's you," he murmured as he sniffed her neck. Darcy gave him a little shove as she giggled girlishly. "It's your dinner, silly. Sit down and eat it."

"Dinner?" asked Kyle. "You cooked? What's the occasion?"

"I finished my writing project! I did it. It's done. Well, actually, I finished it twice," Darcy said triumphantly.

"Huh?" was Kyle's quizzical response.

"Sit down and I'll tell you about it while you eat."

As Kyle stuffed himself with roast chicken, mashed potatoes, gravy, glazed carrots and steamed broccoli, Darcy told him all about her day. She described her elation at finishing up her project that morning. He laughed at her description of her excitement and relief. She went on to tell him about running into Mrs. Lawson at the grocery store. When she started to tell him about her trip to Findley's, her throat tightened and tears stung her eyes.

"Why, honey, what's the matter?" Kyle asked in concern.

"Nothing," Darcy assured him. "It's just that what I am about to tell you is unbelievably special and it chokes me up just thinking about it."

"Take your time. I'm not going anywhere," said Kyle as he helped himself to another serving of mashed potatoes and the last of the glazed carrots.

As Darcy repeated what Mary Anne had shared with her, Kyle kept looking up from his plate. His eyes kept getting bigger and bigger. When Darcy finished the story, he laid down his fork and shook his head in awe. "Well, I see what you meant about finishing your project twice. You had to suspend your deadline and make some additions, didn't you?"

"I most certainly did," agreed Darcy. There's no way on earth I could leave them out-especially Mary Anne's. But now I am truly and surely finished."

Kyle said "That's great, honey. I am so happy for you. He groaned and leaned back in his chair. I am stuffed to the gills. I couldn't eat another bite. Thanks for the delicious dinner, dear."

"But there's dessert," protested Darcy.

"I'm sorry honey but I didn't leave any room for dessert. Maybe later."

"But it's chocolate pudding," Darcy told him.

Kyle's eyebrows raised and his expression brightened. He scooted his chair back up close to the table. "Bring me a bowl, woman," he commanded.

CHAPTER EIGHT

IT DID DARCY'S HEART GOOD to watch the family savoring the Thanksgiving dinner she had lovingly prepared. Jared, especially, seemed to be enjoying the home cooked meal.

"I'm thankful for my mom's mashed potatoes and my mom's cranberry sauce and my mom's green beans and my mom's squash and…….."

"Ok, Jared, we get it!" interrupted Claire. "But Jared is right, Mom. The food at school is edible, but I actually have dreams about your home cooking. We've been looking forward to this for weeks."

"I thought it was going to be kind of hard to get through this first Thanksgiving without Grand," said Jared, " and I miss her like crazy, but I've got peace now about her being gone."

"Me, too," agreed Claire. "At first I felt guilty about getting to where I didn't cry every day. But now, when I think about Grand, I remember the happy times. Boy did we ever have some happy times."

"I'm so glad you kids have such good memories of Grand. She loved you both so much," said Darcy.

"Hey," piped up Jared, "remember the Thanksgiving when Grand lost her ring and Dad found it in the turkey during dinner?"

That opened the gate to memory lane and the entire dinner conversation became centered around Grand and all the good times they had shared with her. Jared recalled how he would pull pranks on her and she would always get him back. Claire talked about all the good books she had read at Grand's recommendation. Darcy almost had to bite her tongue to keep from saying anything that would give away her writing project surprise.

Jared summed everything up as Claire and Darcy carried four pieces of pie to the table. "Well, I really meant what I said at the memorial service. Nobody ever had a better grandmother than my Grand- our Grand, Claire."

"Or a better mother," said Darcy.

"Or mother-in-law," added Kyle, lifting is glass of cider. Taking their cue from him, each of the others raised their glasses as well. Clicking the goblets together, they simultaneously toasted their absent beloved. "To Grand," they all said, "To Grand."

CHAPTER NINE

THE COMPLETED BOOKS WERE BEAUTIFUL. Darcy held them against her chest and whispered "Thank you, Lord." Then she uncharacteristically did a little happy dance. She was so eager for her children to see them. Claire's had a pink cover and Jared's was dark green. Both copies featured the photograph Darcy had chosen of Grand and the kids. The copy Darcy had made up for Kyle and herself had a lavender cover and it bore a photograph of Hannah posing with Kyle and Darcy on their wedding day. Across the cover of each copy, right above the photos, were the words *TELL THEM SO-THE ENDURING LEGACY OF HANNAH MAST MILLER*.

Oh, she was so pleased, so very pleased to have been able to do this for her children and also, really, for her mother. She knew that the kids would be thrilled, and she felt confident that they would grow to heed the admonition which was at the very heart of this whole endeavor. She was going to have to wait until Christmas, though, to see their reactions. That was only a couple of weeks away and with all she had to do in that short time, she knew the time would surely fly.

Next on her to-do list was a search through her closets. Every Christmas she took several bags of clothing and household goods to the homeless shelter. She always enjoyed the gleaning. This year she seemed to be filling more bags than usual. Once she had removed from her own closet everything that she had decided was just too young for her any more, or didn't fit right, or was out of date, she moved on to Kyle's closet. As usual, that didn't yield much. Kyle didn't buy many clothes and what he did buy, he kept forever. He wore suits and dress shirts on his job at the accounting firm and favored khakis and comfortable pullover shirts the rest of the time. His wardrobe was traditional and conservative, just like him. Darcy did find one red sweater that he hadn't cared for and hardly ever wore. He had received it as a gift (from her). She tossed it into a bag with a sigh.

In Claire and Jared's closets she found the bags they had filled when they were home for Thanksgiving and she lugged them out to the car along with the rest. With a little difficulty, she got everything stuffed into the vehicle without compromising her visibility. Her plans were to get everything delivered to the homeless shelter in time to go to the supermarket and refill the car with groceries for the food bank. The shelter, the food bank, Angel Tree prison ministries, and her own church's offering for missions were the four things she and Kyle remembered every Christmas without fail. Additionally, she and Kyle always participated in a fifth activity, this one more of a 'doing' than just a giving. To keep it fresh, they changed it up every year. Sometimes Kyle came up with an idea and some years she thought of something. One year they sang Christmas carols at a nursing home along with a group of their friends from church. Another time they passed out stockings filled with cheerful little gifts to the children in the pediatric ward of the hospital on Christmas Eve. The funniest time was the year they invited four widows and one widower to their home for Christmas dinner. That Mr. Crabtree was ninety-three years old, but that didn't keep him from hitting on those old ladies-and they just ate it up. Such giggling! It sounded like a gaggle of school girls.

Darcy backed out of the driveway carefully and headed down the road in the direction of the homeless shelter. While mentally making a list of what she wanted to pick up at the supermarket, she suddenly realized that she and Kyle had given no thought yet to their annual "Christmas doin's" as they playfully called it. She and Kyle were going to have to brainstorm on an idea right away.

Pulling up to the shelter, she noticed Frank, a volunteer who had been donating his time there for as long as she could remember, leaning against the building. He was smoking a cigarette. As soon as he saw Darcy, he tossed his cigarette aside and walked out to her car.

"Hey, Darcy, Merry Christmas!" Frank called out cheerfully.

"And Merry Christmas to you," she replied. "I see you haven't quit that nasty habit," she scolded.

"Oh, lay off, you old nag," he growled and they both broke into laughter.

"Looks like you outdid yourself this year, Darcy," Frank commented as he pulled the bags out of her car. "Are you and the old man joining a nudist colony?"

"Ha, ha," said Darcy dryly.

Growing serious, Frank placed his hand on Darcy's arm. "Hey, Darcy, I sure was sorry to hear you lost your mom this year," he said softly.

"Why, thank you, Frank. We certainly miss her, especially now during the holidays."

"Kiddo," said Frank-he had a habit of calling almost everyone younger than him 'kiddo'-"you got a minute for me to tell you something about your mom-something she didn't even know?"

Doesn't that have a familiar ring to it, thought Darcy, as she nodded and set down the bag of clothing she was holding.

"Well," said Frank with a reflective look on his face, "years ago I was down on my luck. I hadn't worked in a long time and was pretty much up against the wall. Then I heard about this janitor's job I thought I'd probably have a shot at getting, but I didn't own a single pair of pants without big old holes in them. I knew I couldn't go applying for a job looking like that. So I swallowed my pride and came on down here to the shelter thinking maybe they could help me get hold of a halfway decent pair of pants. I had just got here when a pretty woman-your momma, Darcy,-came in the door all sunshine and smiles, carrying a bag of clothes. Right on top was a brand new pair of men's pants- still had the tags on 'em. She handed the bag to a worker and laughed as she said they would probably be wondering why a widow woman like her had a pair of men's pants. She told them she'd seen the pants in a yard sale that fall and the Lord had told her that somebody at the shelter was going to be able to use them.

"Let me tell you, I had not taken my eyes off those trousers since they'd walked in the door, so to speak, and I worked up the courage to ask if I could take a look at them. Mercy goodness, they were just my size. I asked them how much they were and they said, why, if I could use them, just take them. They were free!

"Well Kiddo, my brand new pants and I got that job and I kept it until I retired. I came in here to volunteer whenever I could, especially at Christmas. I ran into your mom almost every year. Then I guess you grew up and took over the job because she didn't come anymore. But I never forgot her or those pants of hers that changed my life. Rescued me is what she did. No ma'am, I never forgot it. Now that I'm retired I hang out here most of the time, doing whatever I can to help."

"How old are you, Frank, if you don't mind my asking?" questioned Darcy.

"I was seventy-eight my last birthday," replied Frank. "But I ain't never

time like this?" On and on she complained, until the object of her
sapproval came hurrying back into the store, wallet in hand.

"I'm so, so sorry," the lady said as she handed the cashier a handful of
ash. "Between running to the hospital to be with my daughter recovering
rom surgery, and running home from there to take care of my other kids,
it's a wonder I haven't left my head somewhere. I don't know these days if
I'm coming or going." The exhausted and worried mother looked at Darcy
and said "I've inconvenienced you terribly and I'm sorry as I can be."

"Think nothing of it," soothed Darcy. "If you don't mind my asking,"
Darcy continued, "what is your little girl's name? I'd like to pray for
her."

"Oh, WOULD YOU?" exclaimed the mother as tears appeared in her eyes.
Her name is Jessica. Jessica Marie. She had a brain tumor and she survived
the surgery. She is not out of the woods yet, but the doctor says she has a
fighting chance. That's Jessica Marie Jenkins."

"You can count on my prayers, Mrs. Jenkins," promised Darcy. Mrs.
Jenkins mouthed the words 'thank you' as she hurried away.

As Darcy watched her cans of vegetables ride the conveyor belt toward
the cashier, she fought with every fiber of her being the temptation to turn
towards the whining, critical person behind her and give her the look she
deserved. She overcame the temptation, but not by much.

That night, Darcy had so much to tell Kyle. She knew she was talking his
leg off, but couldn't seem to stop. He listened with interest as she told him
about her conversation with Frank. They both agreed that it was too bad
his story had missed the project deadline.

"Oh, by the way," said Darcy, "I gave the homeless shelter your red
sweater."

"What?" shouted Kyle. "I loved that sweater." Darcy responded with
"yeah, right," and gave him an ornery grin.

Darcy continued to tell her husband about her day, giving him a lively
account of her trip to the supermarket, and adding how happy the food
bank was to get their donation.

"I'm so pleased to have those holiday tasks completed," she told Kyle
All I have left is Angel Tree and the check for missions. Oh, all excep⸱
that and our 'Christmas doin's'. Honey, I'm sorry I've been so busv
project that I haven't come up with an idea. We're going to ʜ
of something quick if we are going to do anything at al¹
break our tradition."

forgotten how coming to this ·
back. I'll keep on helping as
every day so people can r
these people can't ever
helped a few find w
just never told me."

"Frank, give me a hu
a quick, clumsy hug and th
cry.

"First hug I've had since n
you, kiddo."

"Thank you for sharing that wonder.
would have loved it," said Darcy.

"Yeah, I should have told her, I guess. Any
Hey kiddo, let's get these bags inside before I get a
the sidewalk with a beautiful woman!"

"My dear wife. Have no fear," said Kyle in a tone of proclamation. "I know how busy you have been, and all by myself I have come up with an idea worthy of your anticipation and awe."

"Why, my dear husband," responded Darcy in kind. "I am most impressed. Tell me quickly. What, pray tell, is your worthy idea?"

Kyle grinned and returned to his normal manner of speaking. "What about this?" he asked. "How would you like to be in the charity Christmas parade this year?"

Whispering Springs had the best Christmas parade for miles around. Many people referred to it as the charity parade because the town charged a $50.00 participation fee and all the money went to charitable causes. Because of that, every church, civic organization, club and business in town, as well as many individuals, were eager to be a part of it.

"Honey, do we have time to make some kind of float?" asked Darcy cautiously.

"We don't need a float," Kyle assured her.

"We don't?"

"Nope. We're going to drive my '54!" Kyle's pride and joy was his 1954 Chevy pick-up truck. He was personally thrilled at the thought of having it in the parade.

"I've never been in a parade before," said Darcy enthusiastically. "I love it, love it, love it! What a great idea," she said, clapping her hands.

"I'm glad you do, because I already paid our fee and got our permit," Kyle said. "If you hadn't wanted to do it, we could have cancelled and I would have just let them keep the fee. But, honey, I'm sure glad you want to. We'll put a wreath on the front of the truck and lay an evergreen tree in the back. I told a guy from work he could have the tree afterwards. This is going to be so much fun! You can dress all festive and I-well, I WAS going to wear my red sweater."

"I'll find you something to wear," promised Darcy. "You just get out there and wax the '54." Deciding this was a hot chocolate moment, Darcy got up and walked to the cupboard. As she passed Kyle she kissed the top of his head and he gave her a pat. She really was crazy about his idea. She was almost as excited for him to show off his old truck as he was.

CHAPTER ELEVEN

Darcy had been right in thinking that the days until Christmas would fly by. She turned her attention to shopping and decorating, with the intentions of keeping both at a minimum this year. The parade was on the Saturday before the holiday and the kids arrived home on Friday afternoon, eager to witness the fun. Darcy had all their favorite cookies baked and ready for them.

The weather on Saturday couldn't have been any better for a December parade. Kyle jumped out of bed and pulled the curtains open, allowing bright sunlight to fall across Darcy's slumbering form. She groaned and reached to put Kyle's pillow over her eyes. He playfully pulled it away from her and said "Get up! Get up! It's parade day!"

After a huge breakfast-Kyle and Jared both claimed to be starving-Darcy and Kyle drove the pick-up truck to the parade line-up site. The wreath of evergreen with its bright red bow looked especially festive against the highly polished chrome of the Chevy's grill. It was from the wreath that Darcy had gotten the inspiration for their attire. Kyle wore a green sweater and a bright red scarf as he grinned behind the wheel of the gleaming truck. Darcy dressed to match him.

Waving enthusiastically both to people they knew and to others they did not, Kyle carefully steered the '54 down the parade route. They enjoyed hearing all the friendly greetings called out to them. Along with "Merry Christmas" and "Happy holidays" there were comments that pleased Kyle immensely. He gave thumbs up to the guy who called out "Too cool for school!" To the people who shouted out the question "Is that truck for sale?" he would holler back pleasantly but firmly, "No way!" Kyle had put a lot of work into his truck and he loved having it admired and appreciated.

Jared and Claire were the first ones up on Christmas morning. Darcy awoke to the aroma of coffee and toast. Slipping into the new blue bathrobe that Kyle had given her the night before, she went to the kitchen and claimed her cup.

"Man, we didn't think that you and Dad were ever going to get up," said Jared in greeting.

"Son, it is 6:30 A.M.," laughed Darcy. "Dad's right behind me."

When Kyle joined his family in the kitchen, Darcy asked if they wanted a decent breakfast or if they wanted to open presents. "Presents!" shouted Claire. "We'll be eating plenty later."

Claire claimed the job of passing out the modest stack of gifts under the tree. After each package had been unwrapped and its contents admired, Darcy leaned forward in her chair. "Jared and Claire, you've got one more gift coming and it bears a little explanation," she told them. "Right before Grand died, she told me that she felt she hadn't touched as many lives or done as much for the Lord or made as much of a difference in the world as she thought she should have. Then, right after she died, people began coming to me with story after story about ways in which she *HAD* touched their lives. But the thing is, they never told her what a difference her actions had made.

I know you remember Mr. Baxter and those ladies who spoke at the memorial service. Well, I couldn't stop thinking about how much I wished they would have told Grand those things while she was still alive. Anyway, there were so many stories and they were so special that I knew I needed to write them down for her grandchildren as a legacy of what a wonderful woman your Grand was." She went on to explain to them that she hoped they would grasp the life lesson in this —that if someone was a blessing to them they would not fail to tell them so. Shyly, she handed her labor of love to each of her children, and the third copy to her husband.

"Claire started crying the moment she pulled the book from its festive wrapping paper. She ran to hug her mother. Jared just looked up at Darcy and tenderly said "Mom, this is great. This is so great."

Kyle had opened the copy Darcy had made for the two of them and held it admiringly in his hands. He'd watched Darcy work so hard on this, pouring her heart into it. He'd heard most of the stories, and she had read segments of the book to him, but she had made him wait until Christmas to see the finished product. He was just so proud of his wife for having done this and so thankful for Hannah, the godly woman who had raised Darcy.

It was the quietest Christmas morning the Carsey household had ever experienced. Usually, Claire would be putting on a fashion show as she tried on all her new clothes. Kyle and Jared would be noisily trying out a new game. Christmas music would be playing in the kitchen as Darcy clanged pots and pans. But at their house this year, silence had settled over the family. Everyone was reading-everyone but Darcy, that is. She was quietly engaged in watching the others as they read.

Jared finished first and said "This is unbelievable!" The others shushed him, so he motioned to Darcy to follow him into the kitchen.

Jared made himself comfortable on a barstool and laid his book gently on the counter. Darcy poured two glasses of orange juice and handed one of them to her son. As she hoisted herself onto the stool beside him, he downed the entire glass. "Mom, are all these stories about Grand really true?" Jared asked in an awe-filled voice.

Darcy nodded. "I have no reason whatsoever to believe otherwise. They all came straight from the people involved. You heard some of them yourself at the memorial service."

"I always knew we were blessed to have her in our lives, but I never realized she'd been such a huge blessing to so many other people," marveled Jared.

"Apparently, Grand didn't either," said Darcy. "That's what I want you and Claire to get from this. If someone has blessed your life, you should tell them-while you still can."

"Well, in the spirit of that thought, thank *you* Mom. Thank you, thank you, thank you for this great Christmas present! You really worked hard on it, I can tell." Jared gave his mother a big hug. "Merry Christmas, Mom," he whispered in her ear as he slid off the barstool. "Merry Christmas to you too, sweetheart," returned Darcy. "Hey, do you want to help me cook?"

"Wish I could, but I think I just heard Dad call me. He probably can't figure out that new computer game I gave him." Jared scooted past his mother on his way out of the kitchen and laughed as she swatted him.

As Jared exited, Claire entered. "Mom," she said, and that's all that came out of her mouth before her chin started to quiver. That got Darcy started and they wept in each others' arms for a few moments until Claire pulled away and wiped her eyes.

'Just think, Mom. Mary Anne didn't get aborted because of Grand! I can't get over it," whispered Claire.

"I felt the same way," said Darcy, "the first time I first heard about it. In fact, I already had your book finished and had to go back in and revise it to include Mary Anne's story because there was no way I could leave it out. I'm *STILL* overwhelmed by it!"

"Oh, Mom, I'm so glad you did that. It makes a perfect last story." Smiling, Claire added, "And you are the perfect mom."

"Want to do your perfect mom a favor?" asked Darcy.

"What?" Claire asked.

"Peel potatoes?"

CHAPTER TWELVE

Aт 10:30 IN THE MORNING, one cold but sunny day in February, Darcy's phone rang as she was running the vacuum in the living room. She almost missed the call. Had she not pushed the vacuum a tad too far and pulled the cord from the outlet, she wouldn't have heard the phone at all. Not recognizing the caller's number, she answered a bit cautiously.

"Hello?"

"Mrs. Carsey?"

"Who is calling please?"

"This is Jim Baxter, Mrs. Carsey. I'm a book publisher. We met at your mother's memorial service. I spoke briefly about your mother's influence on my life, you'll recall. The spelling bee?"

"Why, yes. Mr. Baxter, I do recall," said Darcy. "It's nice to hear from you. Is there something I can do for you?"

"There is something *I* can do for *you*, Mrs. Carsey," replied Mr. Baxter. "I want to publish your book."

"You want to publish my book?!" exclaimed Darcy. "Mr. Baxter, I don't have a book. Not a real book. I just have a little collection of stories about my mother that I put together for my children. And anyway, how in the world do you know about it?"

Mr. Baxter chuckled. "Mrs. Carsey, I'm a book publisher. It's what I do, and I'm pretty good at it. I can turn a small, private collection of stories into a published work that can go on to touch the world. As to how I know about what you have written, you can thank your son, Jared, for that."

"Jared?" asked Darcy, a bit dazed.

"Yes, Jared. He has evidently taken a girl named Hailey out on a few dates there at school. Nothing serious, I'm told. So anyway, Jared went on

50

and on to Hailey about what a wonderful book you had written about his grandmother. He just couldn't say enough about how good it was, and told her that, in his opinion, it ought to be published. Well, Hailey, who is an English major, just insisted that he let her read it. He did let her, and she was extremely impressed by it. She told her mother how moved she had been by what she had read, and that she agreed with Jared that it ought to be published. Mrs. Carsey, Hailey's mother is my wife's best friend, so of course Linda told Pam and Pam told me. Now I'm calling you. You could call it a coincidence, but I sense the Lord's hand in this."

Darcy was speechless. Mr. Baxter had captured her interest with the phrase GO ON TO TOUCH THE WORLD. Wasn't that what her mother had wanted to do-what her mother had felt she had failed to do?

"Mrs. Carsey, are you still there?" questioned Mr. Baxter after a moment's silence.

"Please, call me Darcy. I'm still here. I'm sorry. I was just a little overwhelmed there for a minute," she apologized.

"Well, what I would like to do Mrs.-um-Darcy is to read the lovely thing you have written and then we can decide where to go from there. Would that be all right? Can you send me a copy of your book?" asked the publisher.

"Why, yes, Mr. Baxter, I'll do that right away."

"Now, Darcy, you are going to have to call me Jim," he told her.

"Oh, ok then, Jim, where do I send the copy?" asked Darcy. They spent a few more minutes on the phone while Jim explained to Darcy just what he wanted her to do. After wishing each other a good day, they both hung up.

Darcy moved to the sofa and sank onto its cushions. She sat there completely stunned. After a few moments, she slid to her knees and folded her hands. "Lord," she prayed, "I never dreamed when I started this project that anything remotely like this could possibly happen-but I guess you did. Father, I am leaving this completely up to you. If Mr. Baxter is right about your hand being in this, then I want you to use it-and me-in any way you can. Help me to do my best for you, and help me to remember that Mom would have wanted all the glory to go to you-not to me-and certainly not to her. Thank you for being in control of my life-past, present and future."

Darcy stood up and tried to pull herself together. She was beginning to feel the Lord's hand in this, just like Mr. Baxter had said. There was rising within her a feeling of joyful anticipation. She went straight to work.

Before the day was over, Mr. Baxter's copy of "Tell Them So" had been sent.

When Kyle arrived home that evening, Darcy was so eager to share her news that she practically pounced on him when he walked into the house. "Oh, Kyle, oh Kyle, oh Kyle" was all she could say at first. He knew not to be alarmed, for the light in her eyes was radiating happiness and her face was beaming. When she was finally able to fill him in on everything Mr. Baxter had said, Kyle gave his wife a big hug and kissed her soundly.

"Honey," said Kyle, I agree with both of you. I feel the Lord's hand in this, too. I don't know just what all is going to become of this, but it sure is exciting." Then, being, a man, he asked, "I don't suppose you fixed anything for dinner?"

"Dinner!" cried Darcy. "Oh, honey, I didn't. But I'm thinking I can warm something up."

"Well, I was thinking I'd take my best girl out to celebrate," said Kyle. "What would you say to that?"

"I'd say I like the way you think," Darcy told him.

Over dinner, they speculated as to what it was going to take to turn "Tell Them So" into a real book. Darcy wondered about Mr. Baxter's expectations and whether he would find the book to be as good as he anticipated. Kyle admonished her not to fret about it, but to wait and see.

A few days passed and Darcy kept herself as busy as possible while waiting to hear back from Mr. Baxter. She knew that publishers were extremely busy and that her project certainly couldn't be of high priority. It would surely be several weeks, if not months, before she heard anything.

Three weeks after Darcy's phone conversation with Jim Baxter, she received a thick packet in the mail from his publishing house. Enclosed, was a long letter explaining the procedure that would be followed in the publication of TELL THEM SO. There was also a contract for them to sign.

That night she and Kyle sat down together at the dining room table with the packet of information, a notebook and a pen. They studied everything line by line and eventually made sense of it all. The letter encouraged them to call with any questions they might have and they jotted down several. It all seemed very straightforward to Kyle, an accountant, but Darcy still asked if it was necessary to show the contract to their lawyer.

"Everything looks perfectly fine to me, honey," Kyle told her, "but it's always good policy with any contract to make sure you have an accurate understanding of everything to which you are agreeing. I'll drop it off at our lawyer's office tomorrow and have him take a look at it, but I certainly don't foresee any problems."

As Kyle had predicted, the lawyer gave the contract his complete approval. Darcy signed on the dotted line. She had a book contract! It was time to begin work on the requested revisions. She was so happy they wanted the book to be longer. She would be able to include Frank's wonderful story about the pants and several other stories as well that had come in post-deadline. She would be able to expand a little on some of the stories already in the book. She added things about her mother's life that she had not put in the original book, as it had been written for family members to whom those things were already known. There were a few places where she made things a little clearer for her readers by revising her wording or sentence structure or adding a little more detail. With her enthusiasm for the job, she completed the revision in good time, and found herself very pleased with the results.

By late summer TELL THEM SO was just about ready to hit the stores. It had been decided to release it in November, or perhaps late October, as its theme seemed to fit in so well with Thanksgiving. Darcy was more excited every day to see her book and she was so pleased they had decided to keep her original title.

In early October the Federal Express van pulled up in front of the Carsey's house. Darcy opened the door and practically danced in the doorway as she signed for the heavy box. She hurried to the kitchen for a knife and began to slit the tape securing the box flaps. The thought crossed her mind that perhaps she should wait and include Kyle in this moment with her. Her excitement banished that thought, however, and she quickly, but carefully, finished opening the box.

There it was-her book! She was gazing at her baby for the first time, for surely she had given birth to it. The jacket was a deep blue with the title printed in a complementary lighter shade of blue. Beneath the title there ran a subtitle… LETTING OTHERS KNOW HOW THEY HAVE BLESSED YOUR LIFE….WHILE YOU STILL CAN.

Darcy had ordered copies for Kyle, herself, Jared, Claire, Aunt Sally, Mary Anne and her pastor, plus an additional five copies. Neatly packed in the box were twelve identical books, crisp and fresh and beautiful. Lying on top was a white envelope bearing Darcy's name. She lifted the envelope from the box and laid it aside momentarily. Carefully, she picked up, for the first time, her book. She ran her hand over the front cover and then the back and then the spine. She drew her finger across the title. She held it up to her face and took in its scent. After gently examining every inch of the exterior, Darcy gently opened the front cover. Turning to the dedication, she read the words she had painstakingly penned:

DEDICATED TO THE MEMORY OF MY BELOVED MOTHER, HANNAH MAST MILLER, WHO GENTLY ROCKED HER WORLD-AND DIED WITHOUT REALIZING WHAT AN IMPACT SHE HAD MADE ON THE LIVES OF OTHERS.

After Kyle was able to admire the books in their pristine condition, Darcy prepared to mail copies to Jared and Claire. It wouldn't be fair for them to have to wait until they came home for Thanksgiving, she thought. She couldn't decide whether to sign them or not and finally called Jared to ask for his preference.

"They arrived?" Jared asked her. "You're actually holding one of them in your actual hand?"

"Actually, Jared, I am," laughed Darcy, "and it is just beautiful. Now, do you want me to sign yours or not?"

"Mom," sighed Jared, in a tone of false exasperation, "how many signed first editions of best sellers have I ever had the opportunity to own? Of course, sign it!" She reminded her son that it was not a best seller. "Not yet!" said Jared.

In Whispering Springs, at least, Darcy quickly did become a best-selling author. As soon as the book became available for purchase, everybody in town grabbed up at least one copy for themselves and, more often than not, a second copy for a friend or relative. All of Hannah's former Sunday school pupils and elementary school students had to have one. The book was purchased by all of Hannah's old friends and all of Darcy and Kyle's current ones. Even Kyle's business associates were eager to secure copies for themselves. Tell Them So had soon been read by everyone in town.

Darcy was being asked everywhere she went to sign copies of TELL THEM SO-in church, the supermarket, the department store, the bank, and in restaurants. She was always happy to oblige, although a little embarrassed by her unexpected celebrity. What she very much enjoyed, though, more than any compliments directed at her, were all the lovely things people had to say about her mother.

Whenever possible, Darcy steered the conversation towards the life lesson her book was written to convey. Shyly at first, and then with increasing boldness, she would ask people if there were any circumstances in their own lives to which the TELL THEM SO admonition applied. She was thrilled to hear, over and over again, ways in which people had taken the message to heart and acted upon it. Just as exciting were the many times she heard from people who had become the recipients of words of recognition, appreciation and kindness.

One afternoon while Darcy was shoe shopping, a stranger approached her. The pleasant, well dressed woman apologized for bothering Darcy and then asked for a moment of her time. Identifying herself as Sharon Rhodes, she went on to tell her story.

Sharon described for Darcy how spiritually, emotionally, physically and mentally frazzled she had been by the time she had raised her daughter Stephanie. Nothing the mother had ever said or done had pleased or satisfied the girl. Sharon had lost all track of how many times she'd had to endure the sting of such hateful words as "You don't know anything", or "I can't wait to get away from you." Stephanie left home at the earliest opportunity, and for three years she had not even once contacted her mother. It hurt, Sharon confided, but said that, frankly, the lack of constant criticism and drama in her life had been a bit of a relief. She had felt like an utter failure as a parent.

Then a friend of Stephanie's happened to read TELL THEM SO, having been drawn to it due to some dynamics in her own family. One day the young woman shared with Stephanie her long tale of dysfunctional family history. During the discussion she mentioned Darcy's book. Stephanie asked if she could read it. One morning shortly thereafter, Stephanie phoned her mother.

"Mom," Stephanie confessed, "I have wanted to tell you for a long time that all those problems we had when I was growing up were my fault, not yours. I was a royal pain in the neck. I was willful, selfish, disobedient, rebellious and stupid! I've known ever since I had the twins that parenthood is really hard-probably the toughest job in the world. My pride has kept me from calling sooner. I just want to tell you I know how hard you tried and to let you know that you were a good mother. I was blessed to have you for my mom.

Sharon reached into her purse for a tissue for herself and handed a second one to Darcy. She told Darcy that she was happier than she had been in years-and that she couldn't wait for the upcoming mother/daughter reunion. It was such a dream-come-true that she was going to be able to have a relationship with her grandchildren. Darcy hugged her new acquaintance and rejoiced with her over the wonderful change in her life.

People with all kinds of such heartwarming stories crossed Darcy's path more and more frequently, the longer her book was out. Each time she heard another way in which God had used her book and her mother's legacy to bless someone's life she offered a prayer of gratitude to God.

Kyle had told Darcy that sales would be waning after the initial wave of interest, but they were both pleasantly surprised to see the numbers soar over Christmas and then hold steady at a very good pace thereafter. Darcy opened a special account at the bank into which she deposited every penny brought in by her book.

"What are you going to do with your new found wealth, Lady Darcy?" Kyle had asked.

"God hasn't revealed that to me just yet," answered Darcy, "but to tell you the truth, I kind of feel like it is Mom's money since it's Mom's story."

"Well, whatever you feel led to do with it will be fine with me," Kyle assured her.

"I knew it would be," she replied.

CHAPTER THIRTEEN

ONE SUNDAY AFTER CHURCH, THE pastor's wife pulled Darcy aside. "Darcy," said Sarah Morgan, "we've had a cancellation by one of the speakers for our Ladies' Conference this spring, and it has been recommended that we ask you to replace her. It fact, it was unanimous."

"Speak?" asked Darcy. "Speak about what?"

The pastors' wife gave Darcy a look that had "duh" written all over it, although she was a polite and proper minister's wife and would never have said it out loud. "Why, about your book, of course, Darcy! About the *TELL THEM SO* Movement."

"*TELL THEM SO* is a movement? When did it become a movement?" asked Darcy, a little bewildered.

"When everyone in this church, this community and all over the country, it seems, read your book and started taking its message to heart," Sarah Morgan answered patiently.

"Well, if everyone has already read the book, there's nothing more for me to say," protested a reluctant Darcy.

Mrs. Morgan sighed. "Of course there is, Darcy! Encouragement to continue acting on the book's admonition, reports of results, answers to prayers, all sorts of things!"

"I am not a public speaker," said Darcy.

"Not very long ago, you weren't a writer," answered Sarah Morgan.

Darcy was very quiet as she and Kyle sat at lunch a short time later. "What's on your mind, honey?" asked Kyle

"You won't believe it," she answered. "It makes no sense, no sense at all. They want me to speak at the Ladies' Conference this year. I'm not a public speaker, Kyle. They know that."

"You weren't a writer when all this started, either," Kyle answered.

Darcy threw up her hands. "You sound just like Sarah Morgan," she said in exasperation.

"Sweetheart, it's simple, really," soothed Kyle. Pray about it. If the Lord leads you to speak at the conference, then do it. He'll give you what he wants you to say. If He doesn't lead you to do it, then don't. There's nothing to fret about."

Darcy looked across the table at her husband. "Kyle," she said, "you are a keeper. Of course, there's no way the Lord is going to want me to do this."

Darcy wore an aqua colored suit with a simple cross necklace on the day she spoke at the Ladies' Conference. She had sensibly chosen her most comfortable pair of dress shoes to complete her outfit. It was a beautiful, sunny day and butterflies were fluttering both on the lawn and in her stomach.

There was genuine and enthusiastic applause as she walked to the podium following her introduction. Kyle had coached her not to apologize for not being a speaker. Act like you know what you are doing and they will believe you do, he had said. Darcy took a deep breath and looked out over the crowd of women seated in front of her. What she saw calmed her-smiling, warm, expectant faces, eager to hear whatever she had to say. She laid her notes on the podium and began.

"I'm honored to be here today. I know that many of you have already read my book, *Tell Them So,* and I thank you for that. For those of you who may not know how it came to be written, I'd like to share a little background with you." She briefly told the story of the book's creation, not taking too much time, as she believed that most of the ladies would already be familiar with it.

"I have heard from so many people since *Tell Them So* was published who have told me that they took the book's message to heart. They did tell someone in their life, or in their past, something that they wanted them to know. A man told me he had thanked his father for helping him financially when he was starting up his business. He had expressed to his father how much that had meant to him, and how much he had appreciated it, even though he had acted like he took the money for granted when he first received it. It had meant so much to the old gentleman to hear that, much more than his son had imagined.

Darcy told about two sisters who hadn't spoken to each other in over a year over a silly quarrel. One of the sisters read the book and, applying it to her own circumstances, swallowed her pride and picked up the phone. "I have wanted to tell you for a long time," she said, "that you were right. I just hated to admit it because you were ALWAYS right." A ripple of laughter reached the platform and Darcy added, "They have reconciled and are making up for lost time."

"Perhaps some of you have a story you would like to share. We can take a few minutes to hear one or two," invited Darcy.

A slim, blonde young woman dressed in jeans and a pink sweater leaped to her feet as if she had been hoping and praying for this opportunity. "Please, may I share something?" she asked. Darcy motioned for her to come forward and the girl hurried to the platform. She was quite a bit taller than Darcy and had to lean in just a little in order to speak into the microphone.

"Hi," she said. "My name is Lindsey Wallace. When I was in high school I got a real thrill out of shoplifting. I didn't need the stuff, and I could have paid for it. Don't ask me why I did it. I think it was for the satisfaction of getting away with something. I had a very, very strict home life. I couldn't get away with anything there-and I mean anything.

"Anyway, one day my girlfriend and I were out shopping and I took some necklaces and things. Instead of putting them in my own purse, I dropped them into Angie's when she wasn't looking. Then, when we were leaving, the store security wanted to check our purses. I guess they had been having a lot of trouble with shoplifters around then. My poor, innocent, unsuspecting friend handed over her purse, never dreaming that there was unpaid for merchandise inside. Well, it was quite a scene when that jewelry was found. Of course, Angie swore she'd had no idea that stuff was in her purse.

"So how did it get in there?" asked this huge, mean looking security man. Angie looked straight into my eyes and silently questioned me. I just shrugged. She was my best friend and I betrayed her."

Lindsey Wallace took a deep breath and continued with her story. "Angie got into a heap of trouble with the store and with her parents, too. Nobody believed she was innocent. I think that's what hurt her worst of all, even worse than being stabbed in the back by her best friend.

"When I started reading TELL THEM SO, I got to thinking about Angie and couldn't get her off my mind. At first I thought it would be best to just leave the past alone. But by the time I got to the end of the book, I was thinking tell them ALL; tell ALL of them. So I did. I went to Angie and apologized. I couldn't believe she forgave me, but she did. That's the kind of person she is. I confessed to her parents. I went to the store and confessed there, too. I even went to the police station and asked them how I could get Angie's record cleared. They said she had been so young when it happened and, since it was a first offense, she wouldn't have a record. I was sure glad about that! I felt like a great big weight had been lifted off my chest. I even went to other stores where I had stolen things and told them I wanted to pay for what I had taken. They said it would mess up their bookkeeping too much.

One manager told me to put the money in the church offering on Sunday. I hadn't been in a church in a long time, but I picked one out and got myself there the very next Sunday. I sat in the back and my plan was to put my money in the offering and get out of there. Well, that was my plan but it didn't work out that way.

"During the offering, a man started singing a song and for some reason I just couldn't leave without hearing the rest of it; it was so beautiful. After he finished singing, I don't know what kept me glued to my seat-but something did. And what did that minister preach about? Forgiveness! I'd been pretty pleased with myself for all the forgiveness I'd sought that week, but come to find out, I hadn't taken the biggest step of all. I hadn't asked God to forgive me-not just for shoplifting when I was a kid-but for all my sins.

The minister said that if I would confess my sins, the Lord would forgive me and cleanse me from all unrighteousness. I'd have a clean heart and a clean slate. He invited anyone who wanted to pray to come forward. He said , "Whosoever will may come," and I thought that surely included me. I didn't know a single person in that church, but when I went up there several people gathered around me and prayed with me. I accepted Jesus into my heart!

"Well, I've taken up too much time, but I just wanted to share with you what all has happened to me ever since I got hold of that book. I know TELL THEM SO means to tell people they have been a blessing to you. But it can also mean to tell them you are sorry, can't it? That's what it meant to me!"

As the beaming young woman hurried back to her seat, Jane Calloway, the conference chairwoman stepped up to the microphone. "Thank you so much for sharing that beautiful story with us, Miss Wallace. You have been a blessing to us today." Glancing at her copy of the program, Jane looked up and said "Now, I know many of you probably have questions for Mrs. Carsey, so for the next thirty minutes we are going to give you the opportunity to ask them."

Darcy panicked. Nobody had said anything about questions! Oh well, she thought, this will make sure they don't ask me to speak next year. Standing quickly, Darcy returned to the podium. A middle aged, somewhat portly woman unfamiliar to Darcy raised her hand and Darcy acknowledged her.

"I was wondering how you have handled going through life with the name Darcy Carsey?" the woman asked and then quickly sat back down.

Darcy laughed out loud and the crowd laughed with her. A few gasps were heard around the room. Some of the ladies were a little surprised that Darcy wasn't offended, but it was obvious from her merriment that she wasn't. "Let me tell you," said Darcy, "it's been a hoot!" That drew another wave of laughter from the assembly. "When my husband Kyle and I first started dating, I actually prayed Lord, please don't let him be the one. But wouldn't you know it, we fell in love. I knew he was going to ask me to marry him and in all honesty, I was conflicted. I could not imagine my life without him, but I couldn't imagine changing my name to Darcy Carsey, either. I kept thinking about how much I'd get teased and ridiculed for my name.

It was my mother who helped me get over myself. She said, " Look, daughter, he's a good man-a wonderful man. He adores you, and you are crazy about him. You love each other! The Lord has made it abundantly clear, to me at least, that you belong together. God has a sense of humor, he really does, and you, dear, are a little too serious for your own good. I think God wants you to lighten up. When you tell people your name is Darcy Carsey, if you laugh first, you'll be laughing together instead of them laughing at you. Marry the man!" Those were her exact words, "Marry the man." So I married him. I have had fun with my name and laughing with people about it ever since."

A collective 'ohhhhh' swept across the room, along with a little laughter, and a few ladies even clapped their hands in delight. They had been completely charmed.

"Were there any more questions?" asked Darcy. Several more women responded. Some asked about how *Tell Them So* had come to be published. Darcy loved sharing that story. Someone also asked of Darcy what her next book would be out, but she assured them there was not one in the works. Things took a serious turn when a question was posed regarding a sensitive situation of an unusual nature. It was unfamiliar territory to Darcy and she answered honestly. "The only thing I can tell you is that sometimes it may take courage to fulfill the mission of TELL THEM SO. But courage should always be tempered with wisdom. It is certainly not expected of you to put your life in danger. Pray first and then proceed only if the Lord directs. Let Him reveal to you under which circumstances the telling will bring happiness and restoration, not conflict and pain."

The chairwoman stood then and came to stand beside Darcy. "That concludes our session for this morning, ladies. It's lunch time already. After lunch, you will be gathering together into the small prayer groups to which you have been assigned. I hope you take that opportunity to get to know everyone in your group a little better. Don't hesitate to share your prayer requests with one another. We will meet back here in the auditorium at 2:00 P.M. and be blessed by another talented speaker."

As the room was clearing, several ladies approached Darcy, excited to be meeting her personally. Some of them had books for her to sign. One elderly, white haired lady embraced Darcy. "My dear," she said, "I just wanted to tell you what a blessing you have been to me. You are admonishing us to tell that to others and I just hope that everyone remembers to tell you, yourself!" Just that quickly, she was gone.

That evening, Claire phoned her mother, eager to hear all about the conference. "How did it go, Mom?" she asked.

"Oh, sweetheart, it went so well-much better than I expected. After I spoke, the chairwoman announced that there would be another talented speaker in the afternoon. She put me in the same category as talented speakers. Can you even imagine?"

"Well, of course I can, Mom. I bet you wowed them," said Claire.

"I wouldn't say that," responded Darcy, "but I was warmly received and everyone was very responsive. I wasn't a bit nervous once I actually got up there."

"I knew you wouldn't be. I prayed that you wouldn't be," said Claire.

"Thank you, honey. I really appreciate that," Darcy told her daughter.

"Mom, you didn't fall on your face or anything coming down off the platform, did you?" asked Claire.

"Well, of course not, Claire! Why would you ask that?" questioned Darcy.

"Because I prayed about that, too," answered her daughter.

CHAPTER FOURTEEN

DARCY WAS LYING ON THE sofa reading a book late one evening soon after the Ladies' Conference, when she realized she hadn't retained a thing from the last two pages. It was time to go to bed. She looked over at Kyle, asleep in his recliner. Reaching for the remote on the coffee table, she turned off the documentary that hadn't been interesting enough to keep Kyle awake. She slipped over to her husband and gently kissed the top of his head.

"Honey, wake up and go to bed," Darcy said softly.

"Wha-uh-oh, hey, did I nod off? I wanted to see how this thing ended." Kyle yawned. "Oh well, let's call it a night."

They were just heading for the bedroom when the phone rang. Kind of late for a phone call, Darcy thought. She hoped nothing was wrong with the kids.

It was Jared. "Hey, Mom," he said, "how would you like to move into the 21st century?"

Darcy stifled a huge yawn and rubbed her eyes with her one free hand. "Honey, right now I would just like to move into my bed. Can I do the 21st century thing tomorrow?"

"Kind of late for you guys, huh?" teased Jared.

"It's 10:00 P.M., son!" Darcy informed him.

"Honey," called Kyle from their bedroom, "it's late. Tell him you can talk tomorrow. Come to bed."

Awake enough now to be somewhat curious, Darcy asked her son what made him think she wasn't already in the current century.

"Two words, Mom. Web site."

"Huh?"

"Exactly! Look, Mom, you ought to have a web site. My roommate,

Trent, has set up a business creating web sites and he's really good. He can fix you right up," Jared told her.

"But honey, why do I need a web site? I've got e-mail," said Darcy.

"It's not the same thing at all, Mom. You need a web site," he explained patiently, "for TELL THEM SO. All the writers have them."

Darcy responded that maybe all the really professional writers with a whole list of titles to their credit did, but she didn't think her situation called for one.

"Mom," Jared moaned. "I guarantee you that thousands of people who have read "Tell Them So" have hunted all over cyberspace for your web site. It's an idea that's long past due. Tell me the truth; you've had people ask you for your web site address, now haven't you?"

"Actually, yes, Jared, I have," admitted Darcy.

"And what did you tell them?" asked her son.

"I told them I was too small and too new to writing for that, honey," explained Darcy.

"Well, Mom, tell you what. You get on the computer and check out every Christian writer you can think of-secular ones, too. See if they have web sites and study the ones you find. See if you don't learn a few things. I've got Trent reading TELL THEM SO now, so he'll be totally familiar with it when you decide to go ahead with this."

"If," replied Darcy.

"If what?" asked Jared.

"If I decide to go ahead with this," sighed Darcy.

"When," Jared stated firmly.

"Jared," answered his mother.

"Yes?"

"Go to bed."

"Ok, Mom. Good night. I can't wait to see your new web site!" Jared hung up.

Darcy padded down the hall to her bedroom. After washing her face and brushing her teeth, she slipped into a soft pink nightgown with pink rosettes around the neck. Sliding under the covers, she punched the pillow a few times and then turned on her side. Kyle's back was to her. Spooning his body with her own, she softly asked, "Honey, do I need a web site?" Listening for Kyle's response, she realized that he was snoring gently.

That night, Darcy dreamed about computers. In her dream it was her birthday and the family had thrown her a big party. Jim Baxter was there. Mary Anne was there. Practically everyone she knew by name who was mentioned in her book was there. Jane Calloway, Pastor Paul and everyone from the food bank was there as well. As Kyle led the group in singing the happy birthday song to Darcy, Hannah came out of the kitchen carrying an enormous cake lit with candles. Hannah sat the cake down and said, "Happy birthday, Sweetheart."

Claire grabbed Darcy's arm and said, "Open your presents, Mom," pointing to a huge pile of packages. Jared got up and began bringing the boxes to his mother. Darcy noticed with surprise that the first gift was wrapped in paper that had images of her book printed all over it. She removed the paper and found that the gift inside was a computer. Moving on to the next box, she saw that it was wrapped in identical paper as the first. Inside was another computer. Box after box, all in the same paper, and all containing computers, were unwrapped and piled beside her.

Soon, all the guests were leaving. Darcy was waving good-bye distractedly to everyone, while looking all around for her mother. She couldn't find her anywhere in the house. She was still trying to find her when she woke up.

After a cup of coffee and a cinnamon raisin bagel, Darcy placed a call to Jared. "Son, I've been thinking," she said. "I need a web site."

"I'll get right on it," Jared promised.

CHAPTER FIFTEEN

Darcy and Kyle were sitting at the dining room table discussing Jared's upcoming college graduation. They were so proud of their son and wanted to do something very special in honor of the event. Kyle had thought at one point that he would buy his son a car. However, Jared had recently purchased a somewhat battered, but classic, Mustang with his own money and the boy was awfully proud of, and fond of, that vehicle. While they were pondering the situation, the phone rang.

"Well, what a coincidence, son," said Darcy. "We were just talking about you. Are you excited about gradua….."

"Mom, listen," interrupted Jared. "I'm ok, but I just need to talk to Dad a minute."

"Oh, my goodness, you've been in a wreck!" shrieked Darcy. "Kyle, Jared's been in a wreck."

Kyle grabbed the phone from a white faced, trembling Darcy. "You've been in a wreck, son?" he asked anxiously.

"Well, yes," Jared answered. "But how did Mom know? I didn't have a chance to say anything!"

Breathe, thought Kyle. Just stay calm. "Are you sure you are all right?"

"Dad, I have just come from the emergency room. They put seven stitches in my head, but other than that I am fine. No concussion or broken bones or anything. I'm ok."

"Well, that's wonderful to hear son-except for the stitches of course. So, what happened?"

"Some guy ran a red light and T-boned me, Dad. He crashed right into my passenger side!"

"Was anyone with you?"

"Dad, I had just dropped Claire off not five minutes before it happened. I was alone, thank God."

Kyle's knees felt weak as he thought of what might have been, but by the grace of God had been avoided. It took him a moment before he had the presence of mind to ask, "How is the other guy?"

Jared sighed. "Not too good. He's hurt, but I don't know how bad it is. He was conscious enough to admit responsibility for the accident and to tell me had insurance, at least. I'll try to find out more tomorrow."

"How is your car?" asked Kyle.

"It's toast, Dad. Totaled! My Mustang! Do you know how long I saved up for that car?"

"I know son, and I know how disappointed you must be. But the car is replaceable. You aren't! I'm just so very thankful that you are ok and that you didn't have any passengers."

"Me, too," admitted Jared. Please assure Mom that I am ok, Dad, because I really am."

"She will be all right, son. It's just kind of unsettling to get a call like this. It's the first one of its kind we've ever received as parents. Let's hope it's the last!"

"Well, just be glad she can't see my poor car. She'd really freak then!"

"About the car, Jared, do you have any thought as to what you will get as a replacement? I hope you will consider something rated high in safety."

"You know, Dad, I have been thinking about it and I really do know what I want to get next-if I can find one in my price range."

"And what would that be, son?"

"Dad, I know you won't think it is that great of an idea, but I really want a Mini-Cooper! Think of how fuel efficient they are. If money were no object, I would get a red one with white stripes. As it is, I probably won't have much choice there. I'll just hunt around for whatever used one in good condition that I can find."

"Well, you'd better go get some rest, son. I'll fill your mother in on everything. Does Claire know what happened?"

"No, I thought I'd wait and let her know in the morning. She is going to miss my free taxi service!"

"Good night, son. Let us know how the other guy is, and if you should talk to him again, tell him we are praying for him. We love you, Jared."

"I'll do it, Dad. Good night. I love you, too."

Kyle looked at Darcy and said, "He's ok, honey. He had to have seven stitches in his head, but there's no concussion. He's all right. The other guy caused the accident and is in the hospital." Kyle filled his wife in on everything else Jared had told him. He reached for her hand as he informed her that Claire had been in the passenger seat five minutes before the accident occurred. Her eyes filled with tears as she whispered "Thank you, Jesus!"

"Well, at least we know now what we are getting Jared for graduation," sighed Kyle.

"We do?" asked Darcy.

"Yes, I'm afraid we do-a red Mini-Cooper with white stripes."

"That's wonderful!" cried Darcy in delight, as she clapped her hands together. "That is the cutest car on the road!"

"Whatever," said Kyle as he rolled his eyes and shook his head in mock exasperation. Darcy wasn't fooled. She knew how excited Kyle would be about surprising their son.

CHAPTER SIXTEEN

ONE MORNING A FEW WEEKS after Jared's graduation, Darcy woke up feeling happy and blessed. Everything was going so well! Jared had been thrilled with his new car. It had been so much fun driving it to the college herself, following behind Kyle in his Buick. She believed she liked that little car almost as much as her son did.

Even with as big a surprise as they had sprung on Jared, he had one just as big for them. He had a job lined up, starting immediately. The company that owned and operated the camp he and Claire had worked for the past several summers had offered him an executive position and he had gladly accepted. The company actually had camps in several locations around the country and also put on concerts, seminars, and missionary conferences for young people.

Jared had no way of knowing that he had been quietly observed by the powers that be for a long time. His enthusiasm for his job, his willingness to take on extra duties, his Christian witness and character, and most especially, his concern for the spiritual welfare of the campers, had not gone unnoticed. Jared realized what a vote of confidence it was to be offered this position at such a young age, and he fully intended to do his very best for the company that was giving him this opportunity. He still had an interest in meteorology, but he had been aware for a long time now that God was directing him towards some type of Christian service. When he had been approached with the job offer, he had known in his heart that this was what God wanted him to do, what God had been preparing him to do.

Darcy found herself humming, *I CAN ONLY IMAGINE,* as she fixed Kyle's breakfast. When Kyle came out into the kitchen, he grinned at his wife and observed, "Aren't you the cheerful one this morning?"

"I'm just blessing counting, honey. Jared's got his wonderful new job. Claire is safe at camp. That accident with Jared's Mustang turned out ok. I was so thankful to find out that the man who hit him is going to be ok, especially since he has two little children and a wife. Your job is going well. My book is still selling. You and I have our health. Why wouldn't I be cheerful?"

"Darcy, do you know what I am the most thankful for, out of all my many blessings?"

"What, honey?" Darcy asked with a smile.

"Sweetheart, that would be you," answered Kyle as he slipped his arms around his wife.

"After all these years?" teased Darcy.

"Especially after all these years," whispered Kyle

After Kyle finished his breakfast and left for work, Darcy went to the bathroom and turned on the shower. She adjusted the water to just how she liked it-lobster cooking hot-and stepped inside. Once thoroughly cooked, she stepped back out and reached for the fluffy blue bath towel hanging on the rack. While toweling herself dry, she discovered a small lump on her left breast.

Must be a bug bite, was her first thought. But upon further examination she ruled out that idea. She knew exactly where she had felt something very similar in the past-on the teaching form at her mother's oncologist's office. She was only very slightly alarmed at first. She had read a great deal of information during the course of her mother's cancer experience and knew that finding a lump didn't necessarily mean she had cancer. Nevertheless, it could very well mean that she did. Given her family's medical history, the sooner she had it checked out, the better.

Darcy pulled on jeans and a soft blue top. Moving to the side of the bed, she sank to her knees. Prayer was the first and most important thing, she had learned, when facing any kind of difficult circumstances-not the last resort. Her mother had taught her that. "Father," she prayed, "my life is in your hands."

Over a meatloaf dinner that evening, Darcy said as casually as she could, "Kyle, I've made an appointment at the women's clinic for next Thursday."

Kyle laid down his fork. "Darcy," he said softly, "is everything ok?"

"Oh, I'm sure it is, Kyle. I'm sure it is. But there's a small lump on my left breast and what with my family history I probably need to have it looked at right away," she answered him.

"When did you find it?" Kyle asked.

"This morning after my shower was the first time I've ever noticed it," she told him.

"Is next Thursday the earliest you can get in?" questioned Kyle. "I hate to have to wait that long."

"Yes, I'm afraid it is," Darcy responded. "I'm sure a few days won't make any difference."

Kyle pushed his chair away from the dinner table, no longer interested in food. "Come here," he said and Darcy went to him. Kyle pulled her gently onto his lap. Darcy put her arms around his neck and laid her head on his as he rubbed her back with his hand. They remained like that a few moments, and then Kyle spoke. "It will be ok, Darcy," he said. "It will be ok."

"I know," sighed his wife.

Darcy had never been a hypochondriac, or even preoccupied with her health. She ate right most of the time and was slim and fit, due more to genetics than exercise. Still, given what she had so recently been through with her mother, she found it hard not to think about the lump. She was relieved when the day of her appointment arrived. Kyle asked several times if she was sure she didn't want him to come with her. She declined his offer, telling him there was no need for him to miss work. Kyle knew that if he didn't go to the office in order to be there with Darcy, it would seem to her that they were making a bigger deal of this than she was ready to admit it might be. So, reluctantly, he left for work, knowing full well that he would accomplish nothing there.

Darcy wore black slacks and a gray button down the front blouse for her appointment. She arrived ten minutes early and selected a few magazines from a rack on the wall before taking a seat. Leafing absentmindedly through the periodicals, she kept one eye on the clock. Fifteen minutes after her scheduled appointment time, her name was called.

She walked into the examining room and submitted to the routine check of her vital signs and then stepped up on the scales. She was pleased to see that the scales in the doctor's office weighed two pounds lighter than the ones at home. After another ten minute wait, an attractive, middle-aged man with hair just beginning to gray entered the room and cheerfully said, "Good morning, Mrs. Carsey."

"Good morning, Dr. O'Toole," Darcy responded. His P.A. smiled and nodded and Darcy said hello.

"So, I understand you have found a lump- just a few days ago, is that correct? Darcy answered affirmatively. "Well, with your family history, I'm glad you made an appointment so quickly. That was very wise of you," said Dr. O'Toole. Darcy nodded. "Well. Let's take a look, shall we?"

Darcy had been sitting on the end of the examining table wearing the garment that had been provided for her. With the P.A.'s assistance, she now lay back on the table with her arms to her sides. She tried to relax as the doctor began his examination. Soon, Dr. O'Toole patted Darcy's arm and said, "You can sit up now." Darcy pulled herself up and wrapped the cheerful, yellow flowered garment back around herself.

"You get dressed, now, and I'll be back in a moment to talk with you," said Dr. O'Toole as he and his assistant stepped out of the room. It only took a moment to slip back into her blouse, and shortly after Darcy had buttoned all the buttons back up, there was a knock on the door. "Come in," Darcy called out.

The doctor and his assistant re-entered the room. The P.A. took a seat in the only chair and Dr. O'Toole leaned against the counter. "Mrs. Carsey," he said in his calm, professional voice, "we need to schedule a mammogram and an MRI as soon as possible. We don't really know anything just yet, but we do definitely need to take a closer look." Darcy nodded. He scribbled something on a couple of forms and handed them to her. "Now, give these to the receptionist at the desk as you leave and she'll get everything scheduled for you."

Darcy did as the doctor had instructed. The friendly receptionist, a green eyed blonde not over twenty-five, checked through her appointment book and said, "We can schedule your mammogram for Monday due to a cancellation. That's good news! I'll find out and let you know if the MRI can be done Monday as well."

Darcy left the building, a little relieved that things were moving along. She didn't know anything more yet, and hadn't expected to, but her mammogram was scheduled and that was progress. She'd had mammograms before, of course, and although she didn't enjoy them, she didn't mind them. She had never had an MRI, herself, but her mother had. She pretty much knew what to expect from having listened to Hannah's account of the experience.

Darcy drove home and fixed herself a turkey sandwich on wheat bread for lunch. Just as she took the first bite, the phone rang. Looking at the clock, she thought to herself that Kyle would be having lunch now, too. She picked up the phone.

"Hi, honey," said Kyle. "How did it go?"

"Very routine- exactly what I expected. I have a mammogram scheduled for Monday and I have to have an MRI, too. I don't know yet when that will be, but I am hoping they can do it Monday, as well," Darcy filled him in.

"Did the doctor say anything?" asked Kyle.

"Only that he was glad I came in quickly and that we won't know anything until after the tests. Sorry I can't tell you any more than that," Darcy told him.

"Do you want me to pick up something for dinner, honey?" asked Kyle. "I'd be happy to."

"No, I'll cook. I'm fine. What would you like?" she asked.

"For this to go away," he said.

"Me too, Kyle, me too," she replied.

The MRI couldn't be done until a week from Wednesday, but the mammogram went ahead as scheduled. Darcy tried to be a co-operative, pleasant patient and the technician was pleasant in response. Of course, there was no getting any information from her. Darcy left the clinic just as much in the dark as ever, but she knew that Dr. O'Toole would soon be able to shed some light on her situation.

Darcy and Kyle both tried to be light-hearted for the other as they counted off the days until the MRI. When it was finally over, Darcy enjoyed telling Kyle about what a strange experience it had been. The technician had informed Darcy that it would probably be a few days before her doctor could read the scans and a frustrated Kyle was not happy with the thought of more waiting. To their relief, they got a call from the clinic the following Monday.

"Mrs. Carsey, the doctor would like to see you next week if that would be convenient," the receptionist told her.

"I'll make it convenient," said Darcy. "Just say when."

"Well, he could see you next Monday at 4:00 or Thursday at 11:00." Are you kidding, thought Darcy. What she said out loud was that Monday would be fine.

"Ok, then, Monday at 4:00, then. He'll be doing a biopsy."

"Oh," said Darcy flatly. "All right, then. Thank you." She hung up the phone. She had known there might be a biopsy, but somehow having one scheduled was very sobering.

When Darcy let Kyle know that she was having a biopsy on Monday, he insisted that he was going with her. She told him she wouldn't have it any other way- that she wanted and needed him to be there with her. Kyle wished that he could take off work and run away with Darcy for a week to someplace romantic, but he realized that it wouldn't change anything. They would get from this Monday to next Monday somehow.

Darcy seemed to find cooking to be a way to take her mind off things. She was a great cook and prepared wonderful meals for Kyle all the time. But now she was in overdrive. She pulled out all of her many cookbooks and spent hours looking through them for special recipes. Every night, Kyle came home to lavish meals. He loved some of the dishes, but gently let Darcy know that a few of them were just a little too exotic for his palette. She agreed and promised to never prepare them again. There were more desserts than any one man could possibly handle, even a man who loved his desserts. There was carrot cake with cream cheese frosting, cherry cheesecake, blueberry pie, German chocolate cake, chocolate pudding and apple crisp. Almost every day, Kyle took leftover dessert to work with him to share with the others, which made him quite popular for awhile.

On the day of Darcy's biopsy, Kyle weighed himself after showering. He had gained two pounds! Deciding not to share that information with Darcy, he dressed quickly and headed to the kitchen, seeking coffee. He found that Darcy already had the ingredients for a huge breakfast spread out on the counter.

"Sweetie," said Kyle, "I just don't have a big appetite this morning. Could I just have some toast?"

"Are you feeling all right?" asked Darcy in concern.

"Sure, honey. I think I just pigged out to much on that terrific beef stroganoff last night," he told her.

Darcy, relieved, returned everything to the refrigerator and cupboard. She preferred having a light breakfast herself. She'd just found out that morning that she had gained two pounds, something she didn't intend to tell Kyle.

Kyle had his toast and a couple of cups of coffee. As he left for the office, he promised Darcy he would be home in plenty of time to accompany her to the clinic. Darcy kissed him good-bye and then began cleaning her already clean kitchen. She then scrubbed the hallway bathroom, cleaned out the hall closet and dusted the living room bookshelves. As usual, when she tended to the bookshelves, a book called out to her. With her attention diverted from scrubbing and dusting, she was soon lost in the pages of the book, and the time passed quickly.

At 2:00 P.M., Darcy showered and dressed for her biopsy. She decided to wear the same black slacks and gray blouse she had worn for her earlier appointment with Dr. O'Toole.

At 3:00, Kyle pulled into the driveway. He came in the house and removed his tie. Darcy asked him about his day at the office and they chatted as he drank a soda. Throwing the soda can into the recycling bin, he and Darcy walked out to the car. Darcy opened the passenger door of the dark gray Buick and got in; Kyle took his place behind the wheel. Darcy could count on the fingers of one hand the number of times she had driven with Kyle as her passenger.

The biopsy was not nearly as bad as Darcy had feared. Although certainly not pleasant, it had been bearable. Dr. O'Toole and his P.A., who was now telling them to call her Molly, had done everything they could to put both Darcy and Kyle at ease. They were all glad that it went well and was quickly over. The doctor thanked Darcy for being a calm and co-operative patient. Darcy told him that it was the Lord who needed to be thanked for that; it was because of Him that she was able to be calm.

That evening, Kyle said to Darcy, "Let's watch a movie. Let's watch the silliest movie we've got."

"Ok, good idea," answered Darcy. "Let me pop some popcorn first." In a few moments Darcy came out of the kitchen carrying a big bowl of popcorn and a couple of cans of soda. Kyle had a Mr. Bean movie ready to watch and was waiting for her on the sofa. For the next couple of hours they snuggled together, laughing at Mr. Bean's antics, munching on popcorn, and pretending they didn't have a care in the world.

CHAPTER SEVENTEEN

QUITE SOME TIME AGO, WHILE Hannah was still alive, she and Darcy had discussed in a conversation the various ways in which a person might respond to being informed that they had cancer. They agreed that even though a person might think they knew how they would react, it was something no one could know for certain until it happened to them. Hannah had been amazingly matter-of-fact when she had been diagnosed. She knew that her life was in God's hands and she knew she would die someday of something. She'd had peace from the very beginning.

When Dr. O'Toole called Darcy and told her that the results of the biopsy were positive, that she did have cancer, she surprised herself at how well she took the news. The doctor said she needed to come in and discuss a course of treatment as soon as possible and she agreed to do that right away. When the call was completed, she went straight to her knees.

"Lord," she prayed, "you have never failed me. You have always been there for me, no matter what. I know you will see me through this. If it is your will, Lord, I ask you to heal me. I would love to live to see my grandchildren. But, Lord, I accept your will-whatever it is. Please, Lord, help me to be strong for Kyle and Jared and Claire. Help me to be brave. Help me to trust you, no matter what."

Darcy rose and went to the bedroom for her Bible. She turned to First Peter 5:7 and read the familiar words, CASTING ALL YOUR CARE UPON HIM, FOR HE CARES FOR YOU. They were sweet and precious words to her. They had seen her through many difficult hours and hard places. "ALL means ALL, Lord," she whispered softly. "I'll be leaning on this verse through whatever the future holds. I'll be counting on it-that I can cast all my care upon you-and I will be doing that, Lord. I surely will."

Kyle took one look at Darcy when he came through the door that evening and no words were necessary. He took her in his arms and said, "Dance with me, sweetheart." Their feet didn't move, but they swayed together gently, the music coming from their two hearts beating as one.

Dinner was light that night; neither one of them was very hungry. Later, they sat on the sofa with Darcy's feet in Kyle's lap. "Ok, honey," she said. "We need to decide how to tell the kids. What do you think? Should we drive up to the camp this weekend?"

"We could," said Kyle, "but I don't know if that might be too alarming to Claire. Thinking things are so bad we had to come up there in person to tell her might scare her worse than a phone call. She would probably insist on coming back with us, and we don't want that. There's nothing she can do here; she's much better off being busy there at camp. I'm thinking that we probably ought to call her instead, if you agree. It's up to you, but I think she can handle getting the news over the phone. I'm certain Jared can."

"Do you suppose we should wait until after we've seen the doctor and have answers for their questions about where we go from here?" asked Darcy. "I mean, we really don't know much, ourselves, just yet."

"Well, here's the thing honey," answered Kyle. "The first thing they are going to ask is when we found out about this. We are already nearly a month into this thing. They need and deserve to know what's happening. They are going to want to start praying right away. Knowing Claire, she will have the whole camp praying within a day or two."

"We can certainly use all the prayers we can get. Well, ok then, when do you think we should call them? Do you want to try now?"

"The sooner the better," said Kyle. "Tell you what, sweetheart. Why don't you call Jared and I'll call Claire.?"

It was so hard waiting for Jared to pick up. Darcy almost cancelled the call. When her son finally did answer his cell, he was surprised to be hearing from his mother. She usually let him call her at times he found convenient, since she knew how busy he always was.

"Hey, Mom! What's up?" Jared asked.

"It's good to hear your voice, Jared. Um, do you have a minute to talk, son?"

Jared caught the serious tone of his mother's voice. "Yea, sure, Mom. Just hold on a second," he said.

In just a moment, Jared was back on the line. "Sorry, Mom. I just had to take care of one little thing. Ok, now, what's going on? Is Dad ok?"

Dad's ok. He's fine," she replied. She took a deep breath. "Actually honey, I found a lump and I had to have it biopsied. I have cancer, Jared.

"Oh, Mom, don't say that! Don't say it!" Jared sounded more like the little boy he used to be than the young man he was now.

"Now, Jared, listen to me," Darcy commanded. "Listen. We've caught this very early and everything is going to be just fine. Do you hear me? Everything is going to be ok. We will be finding out in a few days what course of treatment Dr. O'Toole is going to recommend so we'll be able to tell you a lot more after that. Daddy and I thought we needed to go ahead and let you know now, though, what's going on. But honey, I just want to share I Peter 5:7 with you. Do you remember what that says?"

"Sure, Mom. It's one of your favorites: "*CASTING ALL YOU CARE UPON HIM, FOR HE CARES FOR YOU,*" Jared responded. I used to think that the verse went on to say *ALL MEANS ALL* because you never quoted it without adding those words at the end."

"Well, all *DOES* mean all, sweetheart-all your worries, all your burdens, all your fears-everything! I'm going to be leaning pretty heavily on that verse and I want to know that you will be, too. I don't want to be down here feeling guilty because you are up there worrying. Can you do that for me, son?"

"Yes, Mom, I will. I'll try-but it's just so hard. Grand..." Darcy cut him off before he could finish what he was about to say.

"You cannot compare this to Grand, Jared. Every single case is unique and outcomes are bases on many factors. This is not the same situation as Grand's was. Let's just take this one day at a time."

"All right, Mom. You know I'll be praying hard. You can count on it. Everyone here will be praying, too," Jared promised her."We pray together every morning."

"I *WILL* be counting on it," replied Darcy. "I've *ALWAYS* been able to count on you, son."

Meanwhile, Kyle was out in the kitchen with Claire on the line. Just as Darcy ended her conversation with Jared, Kyle called out and said, "Darcy, Claire wants to talk to you."

"Coming," she responded. Oh boy, she thought, now comes the hardest part. She went to the kitchen and, after giving her a moment to compose herself, Kyle handed her the phone.

"Hi, sweetheart," she said in as close to her normal speaking voice as she could manage.

"Mom?" Claire stretched the word out until it became a whole sentence in itself, containing both a request for information and an even deeper request for reassurance.

"I'm here, baby," soothed Darcy. "I'm here. Now look, honey," she went on, "everything is going to be ok. It will be. We have found this plenty early enough that I don't think are going to be any problems."

"Are you sure, Mom?" Claire asked in a wobbly voice.

"I'm sure God is in control, honey. It's in His hands. Now listen. I want you to write something down. Can you get a piece of paper and a pen?"

"I'm sitting at my desk," Claire told her. I've got them right here."

"Ok, then," said Darcy. "Write this down. CASTING ALL YOUR CARE....
"

"UPON HIM FOR HE CARES FOR YOU," Claire repeated along with her mother. "I know that one, Mom. You've been telling it to me my whole life."

"Well, this is where the rubber meets the road, honey," Darcy told her. "We are going to live like we really believe it-because we do, don't we?"

"Sure we do, Mom. And I know what you always say-ALL means ALL," Claire answered. After a moment of silence, Claire said, "Mom, I think I should come home," in a voice barely above a whisper.

"Nonsense! You have a commitment to your job and to those kids at camp. The one thing that you can do is pray, and you can do that right there. You stay right where you are," Darcy instructed her daughter.

"Well, all right, if you say so. Mom, are you sure you are ok? I mean you sound so calm and all. Are you really taking this as well as it seems?" asked Claire.

"Yes, honey, I'm just fine. Everything is going to be ok. You'll see," Darcy answered.

"Can I talk to Daddy again?"

Darcy handed the phone back to Kyle. She stood there congratulating herself on how well she had held together while talking to Claire. She knew that, if she had cried, she would have frightened her daughter and that was something she was determined not to do. It had been so important to her to be strong for Claire and she thanked the Lord for giving her that strength. She was quite surprised that Claire had taken the news so well. She had fully expected the girl to break down in tears, and if that had happened, Darcy would have cried also. Who would have guessed that Claire would have handled her emotions so well?

Darcy's thoughts were interrupted by her husband's voice speaking into the phone. "Claire, honey," he was saying, "sweetie I can't understand a word you are saying." That was when Darcy became aware that there were heartbreaking sobs coming from the phone in Kyle's hand. Claire *HAD* broken down, after all, but not until after she had spoken with her mother. All the time Darcy was trying to be strong for her daughter's sake Claire had been trying to be strong for her mother. That's when the tears began flowing down Darcy's cheeks-silently so Claire wouldn't hear them.

CHAPTER EIGHTEEN

D<small>R</small>. O'T<small>OOLE</small> <small>SAT BEHIND HIS</small> desk, facing Darcy and Kyle. The couple held hands and waited for the doctor to speak. "All in all, things look pretty good," stated the doctor. The lump is very small. The cancer does not appear to have spread. Not a bad scenario at all, all things considered. I think that with a lumpectomy and some chemo you'll be looking at an extremely hopeful prognosis.

"I want a mastectomy," blurted out Darcy. Kyle squeezed her hand.

"Are you quite sure about that, Mrs. Carsey? Would you like to take home some literature and read it, and discuss it with your husband?" asked Dr. O'Toole.

"With all due respect, doctor, I read practically everything ever written on breast cancer when my mother was diagnosed. Even though we have just recently discovered the lump, I've had a long time to think about this. My husband and I talked this through back when it was just a "what-if" scenario, and we've done little else but talk about it since it has become a reality. I really do want a mastectomy." Darcy glanced over at Kyle as he leaned forward in his seat.

"I support her decision," he said soberly.

Darcy's neck and shoulder muscles relaxed then. "This isn't that unusual or odd a decision, I don't believe," she said.

Dr. O'Toole smiled as he picked up a pen and drummed it on his desktop. "Not at all," he replied. "A good many younger women would be reluctant to go that route, but a fair number of women your age and older decide as you have, especially if they have lost a blood relative to cancer.

"Well, then," he continued, "we will need to set a date for your surgery. I am very heavily scheduled right now and it will probably be at least a month. I'm sorry to have to make you wait that long. Most patients are anxious to get this behind them. I assure you that a wait of that length will not have an adverse affect on you physically."

As it turned out, Darcy and Kyle would have to wait over six weeks for her surgery, a seemingly endless expanse of time for both of them. The mastectomy was to be performed in mid-August.

When Darcy had first been diagnosed, Kyle had called Pastor Paul and requested that the church remember her in prayer. Now he called again to let the pastor know when her surgery was scheduled. Among the Whispering Springs Community Church faithful, there were a number of prayer warriors. These intercessors went immediately to their knees, and in no time at all heaven was hearing from them. So was Darcy. Every day she received encouraging and uplifting phone calls. Of course, once her condition became known, there were calls from the curious as well as the concerned. She found the calls from the concerned a blessing, but occasionally grew weary of the calls from the curious. There really was so little to tell, and it seemed like she was telling it over and over again.

Shortly after Darcy discovered that her lump was malignant, it occurred to her that she ought to be keeping a journal. This was a significant time in her life, and she should probably be keeping a record of it. Another writing project, she thought with a groan. One afternoon, while at the craft store, she saw a lovely selection of blank books, one of which would do nicely for the journal she had been thinking about keeping. As she sorted through them, her hand came to rest on one with a blue cover with tiny white dots. Across the front were written the words "CASTING ALL YOUR CARE UPON HIM, FOR HE CARES FOR YOU." Tears came to her eyes. If ever a journal was meant to be hers, it was this one. She took it straight to the counter and paid the modest price on the sticker.

That evening, Darcy took out the book and stared at its first blank page. She tried to decide whether to make her first entry the current date, or to back up to the beginning and write as if she had started sooner. Not able to make a decision, she put the book in her nightstand drawer and picked up her Bible instead. She was finding herself drawn to stories about miracles and healing, not surprisingly, and, in addition to those, she read a Psalm of joy or thanksgiving every night.

Days passed, and still Darcy procrastinated about her journal. "What's the matter with me? Get with it!" she mumbled. Despite her self-prodding, the pages remained blank.

Finally one evening, Darcy picked up the unused book, determined to begin writing. Just as she opened the front cover, it came to her as clearly as if someone had spoken aloud to her that the book was not meant to be a journal. It was meant to be a Blessing Book. It was not to be a record of what was happening to her, but rather a record of how God was blessing her through the experience. Darcy reached for her pen and wrote "My Blessing Book" across the first blank page and then turned to the second. The words flowed and, before long, several pages were filled. She found herself joyfully immersed in recalling the many blessings she had received beginning back when she first found the lump.

"Where do I begin?" she had written. "First of all, with God, of course. What a blessing to be His child and to know my life is in His hands. To know that He truly does care for me and that I can cast all my cares upon Him. There are the blessings of all the wonderful gifts the Lord has given me-salvation, His righteousness, grace, His Holy Spirit, peace that passes understanding, comfort, strength, joy-hope! What a blessing to have Him by my side as I go through this cancer experience.

Kyle! She penned sentence after sentence about what a blessing he was, and always had been, to her.

Jared and Claire! They were such good kids, and such committed Christians.

She couldn't stop writing. She expressed her appreciation for the blessing of having had such a wonderful mother, and for how beautifully her mother had demonstrated courage and faith in the hard places. Before Darcy had finished her first entry, everyone who had called, written, sent a card, letter, e-mail, and especially everyone who had promised to pray for her had made it into her blessing book.

As the days preceding her mastectomy passed by, Darcy began to realize something. The more she wrote in her blessing book, the better she felt. Her attitude and outlook were commendable. Her faith was growing stronger. Her peace was growing deeper. After finishing her entry one evening and closing the book, Kyle asked her, "Honey, what did you write about tonight?"

"Oh, Kyle," she gushed, "so many things! I was looking up some answers to several questions I had about my surgery, and I realized how blessed I am to have so much good information readily available.

"Mrs. Martin from church called and said I was not to worry about you starving to death after my surgery-that her committee had all our meals planned out for two weeks afterward.

"Claire called and said everything is going well there. It is always such a blessing to hear her sweet voice.

"I read the most uplifting magazine article today about a nurse who survived cancer and went on to work on a Mercy Ship. And oh, honey, listen to this." Darcy picked up her Bible and turned to I John 14-15 and read aloud to Kyle; '*AND THIS IS THE CONFIDENCE THAT WE HAVE IN HIM, THAT IF WE ASK ANYTHING ACCORDING TO HIS WILL, HE HEARS US. AND IF WE KNOW THAT HE HEARS US, WHATSOEVER WE ASK, WE KNOW WE HAVE THE PETITIONS THAT WE ASKED OF HIM.*' God blessed me in a big way when He led me to that verse!"

"Well, I would say you certainly have had a blessed day," observed Kyle.

Darcy smiled. "Let me tell you, Kyle. I am beginning to discover that God sends blessings our way *ALL* the time. I mean," she enunciated, "*ALL THE TIME!* Unfortunately, we fail to realize it. Sometimes we don't even see a blessing for what it is. We take so much of what the Lord does for us for granted. Blessings go right past us or over our heads all too often because our focus and attention is somewhere else. Much of the time, the problem is that we are looking down instead of up. It isn't that God doesn't send us blessings; it's that we don't reach out and receive them."

"Many people would be surprised to hear someone who has to have cancer surgery talking about how blessed they are," observed Kyle.

"Isn't that sad?" asked Darcy. "Just because you have a disease or a dilemma doesn't mean you aren't blessed! Remember that song, "He Giveth More Grace"? "We can actually be closer to God in the hard times, because we lean on Him more and rely on His strength. We're drawn to him in times of weakness and worry. And it seems to me that anything that draws us closer to God is a blessing."

"Well, it sure is wonderful to see you in such good spirits. I think this blessing book thing is really having a positive impact on you, honey."

"Oh, it is. It really is. I wish I had a way to tell everyone who is beat down with worry and fear that what they need is a blessing book. Well, speaking of blessings, I am ready to go crawl into that nice warm bed I am so blessed to have. Aren't you ready to turn in?"

"Yup. You don't have to ask me twice," said Kyle.

Darcy completed her evening ritual and climbed into bed. Just as she was drifting off, she said in a soft, sleepy voice, "Oh-and another blessing, Kyle. Jim Baxter called today about *TELL THEM SO*. Sales are up."

Darcy began to notice that, as her surgery date grew closer, more and more people were bringing her copies of her book to sign. She'd autographed a great number of them when the book had first been released and had participated in some book signings in stores and libraries and at the Women's Conference. After a while, though, requests had waned. She hadn't been asked for her autograph for quite a spell. Now, surprisingly, things were picking up again.

One day, something happened that shed some light on the matter for Darcy. She was signing a book for a thin, brown-haired young man wearing glasses. As she was writing the inscription, he mentioned that the book was going to be a gift for his brother. He then made an odd remark about signed copies of books increasing in value under certain circumstances. It suddenly dawned on Darcy what he was talking about and why he seemed to be scrutinizing her so closely. She managed to remain composed until he left with the newly signed book, and then she burst out laughing. He-and others-thought that, if the book was signed, it would be worth more after she was dead! She found that she couldn't stop laughing. Why she thought the idea of people capitalizing on her death was so funny, she couldn't say. Maybe it was because she had no intention of dying, and the joke would be on them.

CHAPTER NINETEEN

MARY ANNE CALLED ONE MORNING and informed Darcy that she had decided to come and stay with her the week following her surgery. "Just in the daytime," she told her. "You and Kyle will still have your evenings to yourselves."

"Oh, Mary Anne, that is so sweet of you," Darcy told her, "but you are way too busy. I'll be fine."

"Look, Darc', you know better and I do, too. My mother had a mastectomy. It's no walk in the park. Of course you'll be fine. But those first few days are pretty rough. It's going to be outpatient, isn't it?"

"Yes," Darcy told her. "Can you believe it? I was absolutely shocked when I was told that I would be coming home from the hospital the same day as I had a part of my body amputated."

"Well, I guess you would have to be getting a lot more done than that to get a sleep-over," said Mary Anne.

Darcy laughed. "Mary Anne, I know you wouldn't have made the offer if you really weren't able to come and stay with me. The truth is, Kyle wouldn't allow me to be alone even if he had to hire a nurse or take off work, himself. So, ok. If you really do think you can spare the time, plan on coming. I enjoy your company so much; you'll be good medicine. Claire insisted that she was going to come and stay with me, but I really thought it would be too much for her. She and Jared will be here for the day of the surgery, but then it's back to work for both of them. I'm afraid that if I was Claire's first patient, she'd be turned off nursing altogether, drop out of school and end up uneducated and unemployable!"

Mary Anne threw back her head and roared. "Well, we certainly can't have that!" she said.

The Sunday before the surgery, Kyle and Darcy sat in their usual pew, sharing a hymn book. Their voices joined with those of the others in the congregation as they sang a hymn of praise. When the music ended, Pastor Paul stood and began to speak.

"We are a family here at Whispering Springs Community Church. When one of us has a heart ache, we all have a heart ache. When one of us rejoices, we all rejoice. As almost all of you know, our dear sister, Darcy Carsey, is having surgery this week. I know many of you have been praying for her and she and Kyle appreciate that so much. But this morning I want us to join together as a family in lifting up this couple to the Lord in prayer. Darcy and Kyle, would you please come forward?"

Darcy and Kyle stood and made their way down to the front of the church, stopping in front of the altar. It was at this altar that they had been married and it was where they had dedicated their children to the Lord. It was at this altar that Hannah and Henry had been married so long ago, and here where they had dedicated Darcy. It was here, at this sacred spot that Darcy, and Jared and then Claire, had accepted Jesus as Savior and Lord. What a precious place it was to the Carsey's.

Pastor Paul looked out kindly at the congregation and lifted his hands in invitation. "Please, all of you who can, come and lay hands on our sister and brother, and let's pray together this morning."

Kyle and Darcy kneeled on the soft, red carpet and rested their elbows on the highly polished oak altar running across the front of the sanctuary. Everywhere throughout the room, people rose and hurried forward. Only those too old to get down on their knees, couples with young children, and a few visitors remained in their seats. Most of these bowed their heads respectfully.

All around Darcy and Kyle, people were reaching out and placing their hands on them. Those who were not close enough to the couple for that rested their hands on the shoulders or backs of those nearest them. Thus united, the sweet sound of prayer began to permeate the building. Pastor Paul's voice rose above the others.

"Our dear Lord, how thankful we are for the privilege of coming before you in prayer this morning. We praise you because you are worthy of our praise. We praise you for your goodness and mercy towards us. Father, we are so grateful this morning that you are always there for us, always listening-always caring.

"This morning, Lord, we lift our sister Darcy up to you. You know her circumstances. We pray that, if it be your will, you would bring healing to her body and restore her to perfect health. We pray that you will be with her in the operating room tomorrow. Be with the surgeon and the medical team. Be with Kyle, Jared and Claire in the waiting room.

" Lord, you tell us in Your word that we are to in everything give thanks, and so, today, we thank you for the hard places. Those are the places where we learn that our own strength is not sufficient, where we learn that your strength is made perfect in our weakness. There are just so many things to be learned in the hard places-trust, patience, perseverance, gratitude. We pray, Father, that Darcy and Kyle will be open and receptive to all the things you want to teach them as they travel this path upon which they now find themselves. As they emerge on the other side of this valley, we pray that they will be better people for having gone through it- wiser, stronger, more in love with you and with each other, more ready to embrace life and more ready to trust and obey you no matter what is asked of them.

"Thank you, Lord, for this beautiful couple. We thank you for keeping them in your loving hands. Amen."

Darcy lifted her head from the altar, her face dripping with tears. She looked into Kyle's red-rimmed eyes and gave him a wobbly smile. The people who had surrounded them were beginning to return to their seats; the ones nearest to Darcy and Kyle hugged them or patted their backs as they left.

Pastor Paul preached a powerful sermon that morning. Although he did not mention Darcy again, his message echoed his prayer. The congregation gave him their close attention and seemed very responsive.

Three or four couples around the same age as the Carsey's were going out to lunch together after church and invited Kyle and Darcy to come along. Kyle said he would like to join them, since this was the last time Darcy might feel like going out for awhile. Darcy thought it was a great idea. Once the group had decided on a choice of restaurants, they all headed to their cars. Thanks to Pastor Paul's relative brevity compared to the other ministers in town, they arrived early enough to be able to pull several tables together.

Returning from the buffet line with a plate of salad, Darcy noticed that Jeff Sinclair was sitting in front of a precariously heavily laden plate. His wife, Jill, was shaking her head and scowling. "Jeff," she scolded, "they would have let you go back for seconds."

"Oh, I fully intend to go back," he assured her. Jill threw up her hands and everyone laughed good-naturedly.

While they ate, the friends visited and caught up with each other, sharing stories about their children and laughing over recent events. No one mentioned cancer.

CHAPTER TWENTY

İT WAS STILL DARK OUT when Darcy checked into the hospital. She had done all the pre-admittance work already, so it wasn't long before she found herself in a hospital bed, clad in one of their infamous gowns. Kyle, Jared and Claire stayed with her until the last possible moment. As they rolled Darcy away, her family stood watching her go.

Returning to the waiting room, Kyle and his children selected seats that looked somewhat comfortable and they settled in. A television set was on, turned to the home shopping network. Claire had brought along a paperback novel, which she pulled out, opened and then closed again, shoving back into her tote. Jared and Kyle began a discussion about sports that never really got off the ground. Eventually, they found themselves just staring at the clock.

They had been there about fifteen minutes when Pastor Paul and Sarah came hurrying into the waiting room. Kyle and his children stood to greet them. As Jared and Kyle shook hands with the pastor, Sarah embraced Claire and patted her back.

"She's gone in, then?" asked Pastor Paul.

"Yes," the three answered in unison. Everyone sat down. Kyle told the pastor how much he had enjoyed Sunday's sermon. Just as Sarah was asking Jared and Claire about the summer camp where they worked, another couple from church came walking in.

"Larry, Jan, so good of you to come," said Kyle, greeting them warmly. Jan had a basket of homemade muffins and fresh fruit, which she handed to Claire.

"I don't suppose you had much of a breakfast, especially since Darcy wouldn't have been able to eat with you," she commented.

"No, we haven't, and these look delicious," said Kyle gratefully. "Thank you so much!"

"Yes, thank you," said Jared with difficulty, as he had already taken a huge bite out of a blueberry muffin.

"Jared, you are way old enough to know better than to talk with your mouth full!" scolded his sister. The others just laughed.

The conversation bounced around a bit from one light topic to another, until Pastor Paul said he had to meet with a family who was having him conduct their father's funeral. They did not attend Whispering Springs Community Church, and he did not personally know them, so he was going to have to spend some time visiting with them. Before he and Sarah left, they all joined hands for a moment of prayer.

Just as the Morgans were walking out the door, in came Mary Anne Findley and her mother. Right behind them was Kyle's secretary. As the time passed, the Carsey's almost never found themselves alone. Some visitors could stay a little while and some had only a minute to spare. The family was given magazines, more food and Sudoku puzzle books, along with everyone's best wishes. As the time neared for Darcy to be getting out of surgery, the visitors said their good-byes. It was just Kyle and his children waiting together when the nurse summoned them.

"She's eager to see you," was the nurse's response when Kyle asked about his wife.

Entering the small hospital room, Darcy's family was relieved to see her sitting up in bed and smiling. Claire wanted so much to make physical contact with her mother, if not to hug her, then to at least kiss her cheek and hold her hand. She held back, though, frightened that she might hurt her. Darcy saw the yearning in her daughter's eyes and said, "Well, hey, can I get a kiss?" Claire leaned ever so gently over her mother, being careful not to jostle the bed, and gave her a kiss on the top of her head. Darcy grabbed Claire's hand and squeezed it. Everyone relaxed then. Jared began to tell his mother all about their time in the waiting room, filling her in on who had come and what they had brought. His praise for the blueberry muffins made her smile.

"Did you save me one?" she asked. Jared looked stricken and she laughed. "I'm kidding, honey. I don't feel like eating anything. She looked at her husband then. "And how was your morning?" she asked.

"About as rough as yours," he replied.

"What do you mean?!" she exclaimed. "Mine was a piece of cake. I slept through the whole thing."

As expected, the patient was discharged and sent home afternoon. Darcy had an uncomfortable, but not unbearable nig. her pain medication as prescribed.

The next morning, Jared and Claire said their tearful goo Neither wanted to leave, but they realized that their mother would a get more rest with them gone.

Mary Anne showed up bright and early, wearing a pair of blue jean a denim shirt with red apples appliquéd on it. "Don't you look cheer commented Darcy. Mary Anne assured her that she had planned it t way. Although Mary Anne knew all about the tubes still protruding fro Darcy's chest, she allowed a very nervous Kyle to explain their care to her i great detail. Then, pushing him out the door, she settled into a comfortabl chair beside her patient.

"Ok, Darc', here's the deal. It is not your job to entertain me or to keep me company. You need to go to the bathroom, let me know. If you are hungry or thirsty-I'm your girl. Just tell me whatever you need or want and I'll make it happen. If you WANT to visit, we'll visit. But if you want to sleep, or read, or just be alone, please don't hesitate to say so. I can entertain myself in the other room," Mary Anne assured her.

"Mary Anne, you are an angel. I'm so glad you are here, although truth be told, I didn't sleep all that well last night and I'd love to see if I can doze off for just a little while," said Darcy.

"All right then," Mary Anne answered cheerfully. "A nap it is. Do you need anything first, something to drink, a pain pill?"

"No," Darcy told her. "I'm fine. I may feel like eating something after I've rested a bit."

The rest of the day went smoothly and the week passed without incident. The food committee brought more food than Kyle, Darcy and Mary Anne all three could eat and Mary Anne put some of it in the freezer. Every day, Darcy felt a little better and both Kyle and Mary Anne were pleased to see her progress.

Towards the end of the week, Mary Anne stepped into Darcy's room and found her writing in a book. Darcy looked up. "Know what I'm doing?" she asked.

"Um, writing?" guessed Mary Anne teasingly, with a twinkle in her ye.

"Yes, writing, of course," agreed Darcy. "I'm writing in my blessing k."

"Your what?" asked Mary Anne.

"My blessing book, repeated Darcy. "Sit," she commanded, pointing to a chair. Mary Anne obediently sat down. Darcy proceeded to tell her friend everything about her blessing book, how it had come about, and how important it was to her. "It has kept me so aware of how much God is doing for me. I knew I was blessed, but I truly never realized just *HOW* blessed, until now."

"Wow!" said Mary Anne. "I guess the title of your next book is going to be "The Blessing Book.""

"No," disagreed Darcy," "everyone has to write their own blessing book. You are in mine, you know."

"I am?" asked Mary Anne. "I don't think I've ever been in a blessing book before. That is so cool! So what all do you write in there?"

Darcy shared with her good friend some of the many, many things she had recorded in her precious book-her salvation, her family, the early detection of her cancer, her doctor and medical team, all the encouragement she had received, all the prayers. She paused at that point.

"Mary Anne, I'm know that you do, but when you tell someone that you will pray for them, be sure to remember to do it. They are counting on it! Those prayers really hold a person up. You can literally feel the power of them."

Mary Anne looked down a moment and then back up, straight into Darcy's eyes. "You know," she told her, "I say that often, and I always mean to, but once in awhile I do get busy and forget. Thank you so much for that reminder. I'll be more faithful to keep my word in the future. I promise."

Darcy went on to tell Mary Anne that she put song lyrics, poems, quotes, and all kinds of things in her blessing book. Just about everything that came her way that uplifted her and reminded her of God's goodness ended up in the book. She tried to remember to include every act of love and kindness that was directed her way. She always wrote about every time she got to meet and visit with any other woman who had also experienced breast cancer. She felt such a sisterhood with each one of them, given their common bond.

"Sometimes," Darcy said, "I'll write about someone just because t¹ me laugh. Laughter is such a blessing, you know, especially v˙ in what Pastor Paul calls a hard place. I'm telling you, M blessing book is one of the best ideas the Lord has ever g˙ way too busy feeling blessed to feel sorry for myself."

On the last day that Mary Anne had been planning to spend at the Carseys, Darcy made a most unusual request of her friend. "Mary Anne, would you shave my head?" she asked.

"What???" shrieked Mary Anne. "You are kidding....right? I mean, surely you are."

"No, I'm very serious," said Darcy. "My chemotherapy starts soon and I'll have one infusion every three weeks for twelve weeks. I am told that I will definitely lose my hair. I read that some women choose to have their heads shaved before they start chemo. They say it is less traumatic to lose their hair all at once than a little at a time. I have given it a lot of thought and that is what I want to do."

"Kyle would kill me!" protested Mary Anne.

"Of course he wouldn't," Darcy assured her friend. "Actually, we discussed it last night. He said that he was fine with having it done if that was what I wanted; he just didn't feel like he could be the one to do it. He suggested that I ask you."

"Great. Thanks, Kyle," muttered Mary Anne.

"Now, sweetie, of course you don't have to do it if you don't want to. It's ok to say no." Darcy paused and then gave Mary Anne her best pitiful, pleading look.

"Ok, ok! When I came here to help you, I said I'd do whatever you needed me to do, and I meant it. I won't let you down now," conceded Mary Anne. "But, for crying out loud, Darcy, I hadn't figured on this! She shook her head and sighed. "So....how do I go about doing this anyway? Razor from the start? Scissors first? What??"

"Scissors first," answered Darcy, as she pulled a pair out of her pocket and handed them to a nervous Mary Anne.

While examining her radical new look in the mirror that afternoon, Darcy decided to call Kyle at work, something she rarely did except in emergencies.

"Honey, what's up?" asked Kyle with concern when he picked up the phone.

"I'm really sorry to disturb you, Kyle," apologized Darcy, "but I just felt you were going to need a little forewarning."

"She did it, then," said Kyle. The whole head shaving thing had been on his mind all day. He had attempted, without success, to picture what his wife would look like bald. She had tried a number of different hairstyles over the years, and even she would admit that a few had been disasters. But bald? He wasn't sure he was ready for this. He knew he needed to be by the time he got home.

""Yes, she did it-under duress," laughed Darcy. "You need to know that it is pretty shocking."

"But you're ok, then, sweetheart? You're handling it all right?" Kyle asked tenderly. It sounded to him like Darcy was taking this surprisingly well.

"I'm fine" she assured him. She laughed as she added, "Just think of all the money we are going to save on shampoo!"

CHAPTER TWENTY-ONE

DARCY NEVER ONCE THREW UP while on chemotherapy, which was something she wrote in her blessing book more than once. There were, nevertheless, a few miserable nights, and she was often exhausted. It was that deep, bone-weary fatigue that bothered her the most. For her entire life, Darcy had enjoyed nearly perfect health and had always been strong and active. Now she felt barely able to sit up and read a book. When she did laundry, she folded one towel, rested awhile, and then folded a second one. How could she be so tired when she had accomplished so little? She missed her high energy level-even more than her hair.

One afternoon when Darcy was dozing on the sofa, too exhausted from doing next to nothing to do anything more, the phone rang. She was glad to hear it. It would be nice to chat with someone. It was probably the one activity for which she had the energy just then. The caller turned out to be Jim Baxter.

"How are you feeling, Darcy?" her publisher asked.

"I'm just so tired all the time, Jim," she replied. "Other than that, I can't complain." She still struggled a bit with calling him by his first name, but he definitely preferred it.

"How many more infusions?"

"One, hallelujah!" she replied.

"That's wonderful! Well, I have a sales report that might make you feel a little better." He gave her some statistics. To Darcy, it was staggering that her little book had sold so many copies and was still doing so well.

"My, that does make me feel good. I don't understand how it is still doing so well," she said.

"The Lord is blessing it," stated Jim Baxter simply. "Well, listen now, I'm going to hang up and let you get some rest. Keep your chin up-only one more chemo to go."

Chapter Twenty-Two

THINGS DID RETURN BACK TO normal, more or less, for Kyle and Darcy and they fell into a routine that was mainly uninterrupted. There were no more health scares. It was actually pretty quiet at the Carsey house, for which its' occupants were deeply grateful. Claire was excited to be in her senior year of college and Jared was finding his new position to be even more interesting and fulfilling than he had imagined.

Darcy was reveling in her deepening relationship with God. She woke up every morning excited to be alive and eager to discover what blessings the new day held for her. She had never been so full of zest for living. She often thought to herself that, even though she certainly had not WANTED to go through cancer, she wouldn't trade anything for the lessons she had learned and the ways she had grown as a result of that experience. She knew she was a better person for having been in that hard place. Most of all, she appreciated how much closer she was to the Lord.

One warm day in late October, Darcy was humming, I CAN ONLY IMAGINE, while making an apple pie for Kyle, using Findley apples, of course. While sliding the pie into the pre-heated oven, she heard someone at the front door. She wiped her hands on the red checkered apron she was wearing that had once been her mother's and hurried to see who was there.

Darcy was surprised to see that it was the Federal Express man. She hadn't ordered anything; perhaps Kyle had. She signed for the parcel and exchanged pleasantries with the driver. Returning to the kitchen with the package, she removed a knife from the drawer next to the sink and slit the tape that secured the top flaps.

"Oh my goodness," she whispered aloud as she peered inside at a stack of greeting cards. Lifting them carefully from the box, she could see that they were beautifully and professionally done. The first one she examined featured a sweet-faced, white-haired woman in a hospital bed. She was reading a Bible. Across the front of the card were the words *CHIN UP; KNEES BOWED*. She opened the card and there she found her favorite scripture verse: *CASTING ALL YOUR CARE UPON HIM, FOR HE CARES FOR YOU: I PETER 5:7*. The word *ALL* was in capital letters. Tears formed in Darcy's eyes. "Oh my goodness," she repeated softly.

The second card on the stack depicted a mother and father handing a set of car keys to a very youthful looking boy sitting behind the wheels of a late model sedan. Again, the words *CHIN UP; KNEES BOWED* appeared on the front of the card, and First Peter 5:7 was printed on the inside. There were a dozen cards, each portraying the same message, but bearing different images. One picture was that of a young woman and two tiny boys waving goodbye to a man in uniform as he boarded a plane. In yet another, there was a row of chairs across a school auditorium platform. In each chair sat a young student with a number hanging around his or her neck. Above them there hung a banner that said *SCHOOL SPELLING BEE*. Darcy had to chuckle at that one. As she made her way through the stack, Darcy took her time and admired each one in turn. Even though she realized that each card was going to be identical on the inside, she still opened each one and read the verse.

When Darcy got to the last card in the box, a small gasp escaped from her lips. In the picture, there stood a woman, startlingly similar in appearance to Darcy, standing in front of a door that said *CHEMOTHERAPY DEPARTMENT*. Darcy could hardly breathe. Who was that woman, she wondered. The image certainly brought back memories of the times when she, herself, *HAD* been that woman.

Once Darcy was somewhat composed, she returned to the box and found a letter from Jim Baxter. He wrote that he had connections with the card company that had made up these selections. He said that when the idea for these cards came to him (or, rather, when the Lord *GAVE* him the idea) he felt certain he would have Darcy's blessing in acting upon it. Rather than first getting her permission, he had decided to surprise her. She could reject the idea of course, and that would be the end of that. He hoped she wouldn't, though, because he thought it had real potential. Jim was eager to find out what Darcy thought, and asked her to call him when she received the cards.

What did she think? She thought the whole thing was wonderful. She thought the cards were beautiful and she could certainly see their potential. In her innermost being, she felt a deep assurance that God's hand was in this.

Gently, Darcy returned the cards to their box and closed the lid. Oh, her pie! She got up and peeked in the oven. The pie was almost done. My goodness! How long had she been sitting looking at those cards? By the time she had washed up the few utensils and items she had used in her baking, the golden-brown apple pie was baked to perfection. She lifted it carefully from the oven and sat it on a rack on the counter to cool. Turning the oven off, she smiled to think how pleased Kyle would be to smell baked apples when he opened the front door in a little while.

Drawn back to the cards, Darcy sat down at her kitchen table and once again lifted them from the box. Sifting through the stack, she found the one that bore her near image. She held it gently in her hands and bowed her head.

"Thank you, Lord," she prayed. "Thank you that we never have to bear our burdens alone-not for one day, nor one hour, nor one minute. Thank you for this beautiful scripture and for all it has meant to me. Thank you for teaching me how very, very true it is. You care *so* much for each of us. You care *so* much for me! Bless these cards, Lord, and bless everyone who receives one someday. I pray that they, too, will learn to turn every care over to you-to lean on you, to trust you in every one of life's trials. Thank you, Lord. Amen"

Darcy wiped her eyes and glanced at the clock. It was time to fix dinner. She carried the box of cards to the living room and sat it on an end table. Suddenly, she had an idea. Clearing the magazines and books off the coffee table, she then carefully stood each card in a row across the top. Smiling, she returned to the kitchen.

Moments before Darcy was ready to put Kyle's dinner on the table, he entered the front door. She had become very good at timing that over the years.

"Oh boy, apple pie!" were the first words out of Kyle's mouth as he entered the house, followed by "Honey, I'm home."

"Good!" sang out Darcy. "Dinner's ready. Come and get it." She knew Kyle would be a few minutes as he removed his jacket and tie and sifted through the mail on the coffee table. He was a pretty predictable guy. Wait for it, she thought to herself. Wait for it. Aha!

"Darcy, what in the world?" Kyle's tone was a mixture of surprise, curiosity and awe.

Darcy hurried to her husband's side. They both sat down on the sofa, and Kyle picked up the card with the picture of Darcy's look-alike. "Darcy, what in the world?" Kyle repeated, still sounding a little dazed. "When did all this come about?"

I didn't know a thing about it, myself, until this afternoon when Federal Express delivered them. Jim Baxter got all excited awhile ago over my *Chin up; knees bowed* motto and said he wanted to run with it. I told him I trusted him and to use it in any way that would bring glory to God. They're really nice, don't you think?"

"Nice? I think they are some of the best cards I've ever seen," answered Kyle. "You know how much I hate sappy cards. These are so moving in their simplicity. I mean, they say so much in just a few words. When I saw this one," he said, lifting the one that had initially shocked Darcy, "I thought it was you! I couldn't imagine you posing for something like this and never mentioning it to me." Kyle looked back down at the card, shaking his head.

Darcy laughed. "To tell you the truth," she admitted, "for a split second *I* thought it was me!" Kyle looked at his wife with an amused, quizzical expression on his face.

Explaining herself, Darcy added, "Well, of course I knew I hadn't posed for that picture, but now days with all the computer tricks they can do with photography…but, of course, after a second I knew it wasn't me. She sure does resemble me, doesn't she! I wonder who she is."

Kyle was slowly and thoughtfully studying each card. Once he realized they were all identical on the inside, he gave all his attention to the pictures. "These are very well done, Darcy," he observed.

"Well, you know Jim Baxter. He goes all out. He included a letter telling us we could reject the idea. You can read it. But, honey, this is of God. In my heart, I know God's hand is in this. I'm going to give him the go-ahead."

"Of course you are, sweetheart," agreed Kyle. "This is terrific."

Over meatloaf and mashed potatoes, Darcy and Kyle continued to discuss the cards and the long road that had led to their creation. Darcy expressed how thrilling it is that God can bring such amazing things out of any situation over which He is given control. Suddenly she remembered that she was humming *I Can Only Imagine* when the Federal Express man had arrived at her door. "Kyle," she said softly, "with God blessing us here on Earth beyond all our expectations, just imagine what Heaven is going to be like!"

The very next day Federal Express once again pulled into the Carsey driveway. The same driver as before carried two small packages up the walkway, and knocked on the dark green door. Darcy answered with a smile on her face and said "Good morning," cheerfully. After glancing at the driver's name tag, she quipped, "If we are going to be meeting every day like this, we may as well be on a first name basis-Bert."

Bert laughed and extended his hand." "And you must be Darcy," he surmised. Darcy shook his hand and then took the packages. After wishing each other a good day, Bert headed back to his van.

After looking at the return address on one of the packages, Darcy wondered to herself what in the world Jim Baxter was up to now. Three packages in two days!

Darcy selected a box and quickly cut the tape securing it. She saw that it contained several things. She lifted a small white box and removed the lid. Inside, she found a beautiful, silver-toned bracelet. The words CHIN UP; KNEES BOWED were engraved on the outside. On the inside, CASTING ALL YOUR CARE UPON HIM appeared. A tiny silver cross dangled from the bracelet. How beautiful, she thought.

She reached into the box again and pulled out one of those inexpensive plastic bracelets that people wear in support of various causes. It also had CHIN UP; KNEES BOWED embossed on it, with a tiny pink breast cancer awareness ribbon on each side of the phrase. Also included in the box were bookmarks, stationery, and pens. The second box contained a t-shirt, a ball -cap, and a couple of tote bags. In the bottom of the second box was another letter from Jim. It simply read CALL ME!

Darcy went to the phone immediately and was surprised to get straight through to the busy executive. "Did you get the packages?" were his first words when he picked up on the call. It was obvious that he was eager to hear her reaction.

"I certainly did, Jim! The cards came yesterday, and the others arrived this morning. I'm so overwhelmed. Everything is just beautiful. This is so exciting. God is going to be so glorified in all this. That's all I ever wanted." When she realized she was gushing, Darcy stopped herself.

Jim let out a deep breath. "I am so glad you are pleased, Darcy. I know I really went out on a limb and got crazy with this, but the ideas just kept flowing into my head. You did say, and I'm quoting you, now-'Use it any way you see fit.'"

"Said it, meant it, thrilled that you did it," Darcy assured him. "So, Mr. Idea Man, I assume you have a plan on how to proceed from here."

"Yes, as a matter of fact, I do. With your consent, we'll begin mass production. I may be a book publisher, but I have a lot of connections with manufacturers. I have connections with the card printers, too. Oh, and I also have connections with the companies who will market these products."

"You have a lot of connections, Mr. Baxter," observed Darcy.

Jim laughed. "As a matter of fact, Darcy, I do! We will get the contracts to you immediately. Let's get this thing going. By the way, just so you know, I won't be making anything off of this. Don't worry about too many middlemen. My only involvement was getting you connected with the right people and getting the ball rolling."

"No, it wasn't," Darcy protested. "It was a whole lot more than that. Your involvement included knowing an opportunity to glorify God when you saw one and unselfishly working to magnify that opportunity so that who knows how many people may find God's peace in the midst of difficult circumstances."

"Well, uh, ok-but you came up with the motto!" said Jim.

"I didn't even do that, protested Darcy. "God gave it to me. Hey, Jim, while I still have you on the line, what's the story on my look-alike on the greeting card?"

"Oh," said Jim, "I knew that would get your attention. It was the coolest thing. I had a meeting with a teenager who survived a plane crash and wanted to write a book about it. He brought his grandmother along with him. For a second I thought I was looking at you!"

"Grandmother!" sputtered Darcy. "She's a grandmother? Of a TEENAGER?"

Jim laughed. "Yes, she is. She's actually quite a bit older than you, but she sure doesn't look it. When I asked her to participate in my little surprise, she was thrilled to be a part of it."

The next morning after Kyle left for work, Darcy gathered up all the items Jim Baxter had sent to them and carried everything out to her car. She slipped a worship CD into her player and sang along as she drove to Mary Anne's house. Mary Anne was delighted to see her friend. After greetings and hugs, she couldn't wait to find out what had brought Darcy over this morning. Darcy was so obviously bristling with excitement that it had to be something wonderful.

"Sit down and start talking," ordered Mary Anne. "I'll fix us a cup of tea." Darcy placed her boxes on the table and sat down.

As Mary Anne was pulling a pair of cups out of the cabinet, Darcy asked her if she remembered the motto that had come to her when she discovered she had cancer.

"Sure," answered Mary Anne, as she placed the cups on the counter next to the stove. "*CHIN UP; KNEES BOWED.*" I've told myself that more than once since you shared it with me."

Darcy began at the beginning and shared with her friend the whole story behind the contents of the boxes she had brought with her. When Mary Anne carried the steaming cups of herbal tea to the table and sat down, Darcy handed her the packet of greeting cards. Mary Anne's eyes grew moist.

"Aren't they beautiful?" asked Darcy.

"Oh, Darcy, they're gorgeous!" Mary Anne exclaimed. She examined each card, commenting over and over again about how wonderful they were. Suddenly, she stopped in mid-sentence and clapped her hand over her mouth. Darcy laughed. Removing her hand, Mary Anne said "I thought it was you-but it isn't! She sure looks like you." The two ladies laughed together as Darcy filled Mary Anne in about her grandmother look-alike.

After Mary Anne had seen all the cards and expressed her unreserved approval of each one, Darcy returned them to the box. Next she pulled out the bracelet. Oh, my goodness-it's beautiful," murmured Mary Anne.

"It's yours," said Darcy as she extended her hand.

"Oh, I couldn't. It's yours, Darcy," protested Mary Anne.

"There will be more. I want you to have this. It is the first one. Please accept it," encouraged Darcy. "Please."

Mary Anne held out her arm and Darcy fastened the bracelet around her wrist. As Mary Anne sat staring at it, a huge smile lit up her face. "I will cherish it forever," she told her friend.

Darcy explained that Jim had told her that the bracelets were sterling silver, but there would be a less expensive one available as well. They could be purchased with the dangling cross or a dangling breast cancer ribbon. He was having one made up special for Darcy which would have both.

Mary Anne got to see everything else Darcy had brought and before they knew it, the morning had flown by. Not ready to end their visit, Mary Anne fixed ham sandwiches on whole wheat bread and made some more tea.

"Darcy, are the sales from all this merchandise going to generate a lot of money?" asked Mary Anne.

"That's something we have barely begun to talk about," admitted Darcy. "I don't know what the retail prices of these items are going to be, and it's probably too early to even think about sales projections. Kyle and I do agree, though, that any income from this is going into the *Tell Them So* account. What we don't know yet," laughed Darcy, "is what the account is for. God is building it and it is growing, though, so it must be for something big."

"The bigger the better," declared Mary Anne. "After all, we serve a great big God!"

Darcy insisted she had to be going and just before she left, Mary Anne said, "Oh, hey, I meant to tell you that I just read a really good book. Let me send it with you." She hurried to the bedroom and returned carrying a small hardback book, which she handed to Darcy. Glancing at the cover, Darcy saw the adorable faces of some very small black children. She noted that the book was about orphans in Uganda.

"Thanks, sweetie," Darcy told her friend. "I'll get it back to you," she said as she started her car. Mary Anne stood and waved as Darcy drove off.

CHAPTER TWENTY-THREE

DARCY FINISHED READING THE BOOK that Mary Anne had loaned her and laid it gently in her lap. Her shoulders were shaking as she sobbed. Seldom had she been so profoundly moved by a book. She was shaken to her very core. How she ached for those precious children, orphans most of them, who had barely any prospects for a future that was anything but bleak. Without an education, there was practically no hope of them rising above their current circumstances. It cost so little to go to school in Uganda by Darcy's reckoning, and yet to these children it was far beyond their reach-a fortune.

Darcy thought about her own children. She could remember so clearly the first day of kindergarten for each of them-their new outfits, new shoes, cute little backpacks. She recalled how excited and eager they had been as they entered the beautiful, clean, safe building where they would receive a quality education. Her kids had enjoyed every possible educational opportunity. They had gone to great schools with top-notch teachers. They'd had computers and access to an outstanding library. Claire had had that tutor in math her first year of high school. There had never been any question as to whether they would be able to go college. How sad, thought Darcy, how tragic, that so many of the world's children would have little, if any, opportunity to experience the open doors an education could mean to them.

Suddenly, into Darcy's mind, heart and soul there swept a knowing, a knowing so clear and certain that there was not the slightest shadow of doubt. What she now knew made her almost delirious with joy. Thank you, Lord. Thank you Lord. Thank you, Lord she repeated over and over again in her mind. It had now been revealed to her in crystal clarity what was to be done with the money in the Tell Them So account, and it was perfect.

Perfect! She danced around the room. She could hardly wait to tell Kyle-and Jared, Claire, Mary Anne, Pastor Paul-oh, she wanted to tell everyone! They would all be so thrilled. Oh, and Jim Baxter, she thought. Wouldn't he be excited? What a wonderful role he had played in all of this, with his great ideas, and the way he had helped the bank account to swell.

It never once crossed Darcy's mind that she should be worried over the fact that she knew absolutely nothing regarding what she was about to do. Her heart was too full to leave any room for worry. God would lead the way. He would open every door and show her what to do and how to do it. His hand had been in this from the beginning and it would be in it all the way. Wasn't God wonderful!

Darcy hoped that, when she sat down to talk to Kyle, she would be able to express her vision clearly. As it turned out, nothing could have been easier. The longer she talked, the more enthused he became. He nodded in agreement to everything she said. The Lord was planting in Kyle's heart the same vision that had consumed Darcy.

The Carseys scheduled an appointment with Pastor Paul, and when the time came, they walked into his office holding hands. The minister motioned for them to be seated in the comfortable chairs that faced his desk. After sitting down, himself, Pastor Paul looked at their beaming faces and said, "I don't know what's up with you two, but it's something good. I can certainly see that. It's rare for me to have such excited, happy faces in my office-refreshing, really! Now somebody let me in on the fun-quick!"

Darcy and Kyle looked at each other, and Kyle said, "You go first."

Talking with her hands, standing up and sitting down several times, and walking around the room, Darcy dramatically described for the pastor what the Lord had laid on her heart. She spoke in glowing terms of the scope of the vision. When she finally wound down, she patted Kyle's hand and he took over. With less drama, but no less fervor, he honed in on some of the specifics they had in mind.

Pastor Paul had not been so moved in a long time. He was excited over everything he had just heard and was eager to be a prayer partner in such as ambitious project. I'm just thrilled," he told Kyle and Darcy. "I only have one question. Where do you begin?"

The couple looked at each other with startled expressions and then laughed together. "That's the question we had for you, Pastor. Where DO we begin? We were hoping you would know!"

Pastor Paul thought for a moment. "Let me do a little research," he told them. "Meanwhile, I have a mailing address and an e-mail address, as well, for a young, missionary couple serving in Uganda right now-Ed and

Andrea Hardesty. I'm sure they will be delighted to hear from you. They may be the source of some valuable information and advice."

"Oh, thank you, Pastor Paul," said Darcy. Kyle voiced his appreciation as well.

"Keep me posted on any developments. I'll be sure to let you know everything I can find out," the pastor told them.

"We will," promised Darcy. Then she suddenly remembered something. "By the way, there is one other thing we haven't mentioned yet. I've been thinking about doing this rather quietly and surprising Jared and Claire farther down the road. Do you think that is a good idea? Do you even think it is possible?"

Pastor Paul took a moment to reply. "Well, as far as being possible, I suppose it is, especially since they aren't at home. There are going to be a good number of people in the know on the other side of the Atlantic, obviously, but you can at least try to keep it quiet on this side. As far as it being a good idea, the only problem I can see is how hard it is going to be on you not to say anything."

"You've got that right," said Darcy. "It is going to be so hard, I know. Maybe we won't be able to pull it off, but we think we are going to try."

That very night, Kyle e-mailed the Hardesty's. Introducing himself and Darcy, he gave them a brief outline of their plans. He promised that a letter explaining everything in much greater detail would be sent to them promptly. Darcy immediately got to work on the letter and mailed it the next morning in a package that also contained a copy of Tell Them So, gifts from the Chin up; knees bowed line, and also a contribution to the Hardesty's own work there on the mission field.

Within a few days, Kyle received a response from Ed Hardesty. Apologizing for not returning his e-mail sooner, Ed explained that his internet service was unreliable on the best of days and nonexistent on the others. He and Andrea were looking forward to hearing the Carsey's whole story, and eager to be of assistance in any way possible. Included in the e-mail were the names and addresses of several officials with whom the Carseys would eventually be in contact.

"Well, honey, a lot has happened in a short time," Kyle said to his wife that night.

"Can you believe it? We're already in contact with someone in Uganda! The Hardesty's seem so nice. This is going to be the adventure of a lifetime, Kyle." Darcy hugged herself and then jumped up and ran to her husband to hug him as well.

Chapter Twenty-Four

Pastor Paul phoned Darcy one afternoon and shared with her several pieces of information that he had gleaned from various sources-work and witness teams, mission boards, web sites, and companies that had been involved in projects on foreign soil. He had been very busy, and he hoped that the information would be useful.

"Thank you so much for all your work, Pastor," said Darcy. "This is wonderful. Kyle will be so pleased to get all this."

After a slight pause, Pastor Paul asked, "Darcy, are you still certain you want to keep this a secret? The reason I ask is that there are several people from right here at Whispering Springs Community Church who are just itching to be involved in such a project. They would be honored to be a part of this, and they could be very helpful to you."

"Um, let me sit down with Kyle tonight and talk about that. What you say makes a lot of sense. I'll get right back with you on that."

That evening, over a dinner of oven baked chicken, rice and asparagus, Darcy discussed with Kyle the point that Pastor Paul had made. "He didn't exactly suggest it, Kyle. He just sort of put the idea out there. But I could tell he thinks it would be a good idea. So what do *you* think, honey?"

"Truthfully, Darcy, I think it makes a lot of sense on many levels. It would certainly make things easier, and it would be really something for our own church to be involved," Kyle replied.

"If we were to go that route, *Tell Them So* would take care of all their travel expenses," said Darcy.

"Absolutely," Kyle said in agreement. He was already thinking of the men in their church and wondering which of them might be interested in participating.

"Then, are you saying we should do it?" questioned Darcy.

Kyle responded thoughtfully. "The only drawback is that I know you had your heart set on this being a surprise. I don't want a single thing about this project to disappoint you."

"Well," Darcy shrugged, "maybe I didn't think that surprise idea through very well. Let's go back in and talk to the pastor about what all would be involved with having our own church sending a work team over."

"I think that is a great idea, dear," said Kyle.

The very next morning, Kyle and Darcy drove to Pastor Paul's office in separate vehicles, so that Kyle could go straight to work from the church.

"So," said Darcy, immediately upon being seated, "tell us some more about this work team idea."

"Would you like some coffee first?" asked the pastor. "I have doughnuts." Kyle said yes to both the coffee and the doughnuts, but Darcy declined. She was a woman on a mission with a one track mind. Anything not directly related to that mission seemed unnecessary.

"All right" said the pastor after pouring two cups of coffee and opening the doughnut box, "I have something for you. He lifted a large file from his desk and handed it to Kyle, who flipped it open with curiosity.

"These are reports from several projects in which this church and some others have been involved. I have a pastor friend whose church must hold some kind of world record for mission projects. I've included much of the information and advice he gave me in the file you are holding, Kyle."

"Thank you so much for your time and trouble, Pastor. You have been so helpful," said Kyle.

"No trouble at all," insisted the minister. "You don't know how excited it makes me to be a part of this."

Darcy leaned forward in her seat and started to tell her pastor that she was beginning to see how impractical the idea of secrecy about this project had been. She told him that she loved surprises so much, herself, that it gave her great pleasure to plan surprises for her children-and this would have been such a huge one. Nevertheless, doing things that way would present a lot of challenges that were probably unnecessary. "In fact," she concluded, "I've decided to give up the surprise idea."

Kyle looked relieved; the pastor looked pleased. "Oh, said Darcy, "there is absolutely one thing about our plans I would love so much to keep secret for now, if it's at all possible. She confided her wishes to Paul, who said that he saw no reason why that wouldn't be all right. Darcy was thrilled. Covering her cheeks with her hands, she said, "Praise the Lord!"

Kyle and Darcy left the office then and headed for the parking lot. Kyle walked toward his Buick and waved to Darcy, who was already backing her car out of its slot. Kyle thought to himself that his wife must be in a hurry and wondered why. He hoped she would drive carefully, but wasn't really concerned. Darcy ALWAYS drove carefully. She had a better driving record than he did.

Darcy, who had never been in an accident in her life, except for one fender-bender in which she had not been at fault, did drive carefully home. She may have been going a few miles per hour faster than what was usual for her, but that still kept her under the speed limit. When she arrived at the house, she pulled into the driveway and hopped out of the car, leaving the engine running. Hurrying to the front door, she retrieved her extra house key from a compartment in her purse and let herself in.

Mary Anne's book lay on the coffee table. Scooping it up, Darcy headed back out the door, pulling it locked behind her. She jumped back into the car, threw it into reverse, and backed out of the driveway. Now that the secretiveness of her project had been abandoned, she couldn't wait to share everything with Mary Anne. Of all the people she was eager to tell about it, Mary Anne was first on the list-behind Jared and Claire of course. But right now she wanted to tell somebody in person. Actually, she NEEDED to tell someone in person before she burst!

Arriving at Mary Anne's house, Darcy was pleased to see her friend's car in the driveway. She knew she should have called first, not just to make sure she was home, but to ask if it was all right to come over so early. It wasn't like Darcy to just drop in on people, especially at this hour of the morning. Fortunately, Mary Anne was such a flexible, easy-going person that Darcy felt certain she wouldn't mind the unannounced visit.

As Darcy approached Mary Anne's front porch, the front door flew open. There stood Mary Anne dressed in blue jeans and a long-sleeved, red checkered shirt. "Darcy!" she called out pleasantly. "What a nice surprise. Get in here, girl. Come in!"

As Darcy stepped into the front entry of her friend's cute little cottage, she sniffed the air. "What is that heavenly smell?" she asked.

"I made apple fritters; I must have known you were coming. Now, you have to have some or you'll hurt my feelings," Mary Anne insisted.

"Well, I certainly wouldn't want to do that," Darcy said, thankful that she had declined the doughnuts earlier.

"Good. Now, will you be having tea or hot cider with them?"

"Um, tea, I think," answered Darcy as she pulled out one of Mary Anne's kitchen chairs.

Sitting at the kitchen table, nibbling the delicious fritters and sipping tea, the two ladies chatted a bit, but not for long. After a few minutes, Mary Anne said "Ok, girlfriend, you are about to explode. What brought you over here so early in the morning besides the prospects of my apple fritters?"

"Oh, Mary Anne! Do you remember when you asked me about the money that *Tell Them So* and *Chin Up* were bringing in? I told you that God was building that account for some special reason, but I didn't know what yet." Mary Anne nodded, eager to hear more.

"Well, you loaned me that book on Uganda and-oh, good grief, I left it in the car." She pushed back her chair, as if she were about to go get the book. Mary Anne pointed at her friend and motioned for her to stay put.

"You can get it later," she said. "Keep talking."

Darcy leaned forward and began to tell Mary Anne about the day she had read the stirring and emotional book.

"Oh, honey, it gripped my heart! I kept thinking about how much those sweet children needed and deserved an education." Darcy tried to find the words to describe for her what it had been like when the Lord had unveiled His plan. It had been so supernatural, so sacred, so moving, that she found it hard to put into words. Both women were in tears as Darcy shared about the beautiful experience.

"We are going to build a school in Uganda!" exclaimed Darcy. "A school! Isn't that perfect? Wouldn't Mother be thrilled? And not only that, Mary Anne- we are going to fill it with everything a modern school needs- desks, chairs, maps, globes, books, science equipment and art supplies- everything. Oh- and there is going to be a playground, Mary Anne, a playground! And a kitchen, too." Darcy broke down and couldn't speak. She saw through her tears that Mary Anne was crying, too.

They sat there for a spell, both Mary Anne and Darcy unable to speak. Finally, Darcy broke the silence. "Well? What do you think?" she asked.

"Oh Darc', it's so wonderful! It really is the perfect thing. Just think. All this time God has been blessing and using *Tell Them So* and *Chin Up* and now all those children are going to reap the benefits. Did you have any idea that this was that the Lord had in mind?"

"None!" declared Darcy. "No idea at all. There were some many directions God could have gone with this that I didn't even try to guess what His plans might be. If I would have had some guesses, I might have grown too fond of one of them. No, I wanted this to be God's will, and I wanted to be surprised. Well, I certainly am!" Darcy then said that she had initially planned on doing this in secret so that, when the project was finished, she could surprise her children. She explained that she had come to realize how impractical that idea was.

"By the way, except for Kyle, Pastor Paul and me, you are the very first person to know about this!"

"I am?" asked Mary Anne gleefully. Darcy nodded.

"Of course, that won't be for long. Now it looks like a work team from our own Whispering Springs Community Church is going to go over and build the school! Pastor Paul feels confident we can put a good team together."

"Well, I'm going," declared Mary Anne. Darcy looked completely taken by surprise.

"You would do that?"

"Try and stop me," answered the feisty and determined Mary Anne.

Darcy grinned. "Well, ok. I guess they do have women on work teams now."

Mary Anne laughed. "Lady, you really DO need to move into the twenty-first century, don't you!"

As Darcy began clearing the kitchen table, Mary Anne asked "Darcy, your kids don't make it home that much, isn't that right?" Darcy responded that no, unfortunately, they did not. She explained that for the last several years they had either been away at college or at their summer camp jobs. They were home for Thanksgiving and Christmas and maybe Easter. She and Kyle had always tried to make it up to the camp for a week-end or two, but the kids were always too busy to spare them much time. She admitted that she missed them, but said she was proud of them and thankful for the way God had been using them every summer to be a blessing to other young people. "Why do you ask?" she wondered.

"Well….." said Mary Anne, "I was just thinking. The only way Jared and Claire know much of anything about what goes on around here is through you and Kyle. Maybe it WOULD be possible to keep them in the dark, even if there ARE people around here who do know what is going on. That was really the whole reason you wanted to be secretive anyway-to surprise the kids. So go ahead and keep your secret-only just from them. It might work."

"Wow! I think you might be right," said Darcy. "If somebody spilled the beans or they found out about everything somehow, we could just tell them the truth- we had wanted to surprise them and it didn't work out that way. Actually, it is going to be a huge surprise whenever they do find out about it, whether it is when I want or sooner."

"Exactly!" cried Mary Anne

CHAPTER TWENTY-FIVE

THANKS TO ED AND ANDREA Hardesty, Kyle had been in communication with a Ugandan organization that was going to be working hand-in-hand with the Whispering Springs team on the school building project. Kyle had realized that finding a location for the school was the first priority. He and Darcy wanted the school to be in a place where it would benefit as many children as possible and yet remote enough that it would reach children who had no other school anywhere near them. With assistance from the Ugandans and from Eddie and Andrea Hardesty, a site was soon secured.

The next order of business was permits. Having native Ugandans involved in the project expedited that part of the project. There was much rejoicing when the Carseys were given the green light to proceed with their plans. Darcy would sit and study a map of Uganda, tapping her finger on the area where the school would eventually be.

Meanwhile, Pastor Paul had been extremely busy assembling a team of workers. Rather than make a public request for volunteers and then have to turn some away, he had gone directly to certain individuals who he knew to be good prospects. They had skills; they had passports; they would probably be able to take the time off.

William Crane was a talented carpenter. Due to a sizeable, unexpected inheritance, he had retired early so that he would be free to be involved with Habitat for Humanity and with mission projects. Pastor Paul knew he would jump at the chance to be included.

Philip Grant was a concrete man. He owned his own business and could take time off whenever he had a good reason. He would think this was a very good reason.

Bob Jamison was a jack-of-all trades and a general handyman with a better than average acquaintance with all aspects of construction. He would never have been able to go if he'd had to cover his own expenses, but with the Carseys buying his ticket he would be thrilled to be considered for the team.

Tom Lister was a contractor who had years of experience in construction and too much time on his hands because business had been slow. He needed an outlet for his energy. He had mentioned to Pastor Paul just a few weeks ago that if anything needed repaired around the church or the parsonage, he would be glad for something useful to do. Naturally, he was on the pastor's short list.

When Kyle and Darcy were given the names of these men and their credentials, they gladly approved each one. "And don't forget that Mary Anne is going," Darcy reminded the two men.

"And what is Mary Anne going to be doing?" asked the pastor.

"Anything and everything! Sweeping, fetching, holding ladders, you name it. And don't forget P.R. She's fantastic at public relations. I guarantee you, the team will be happy to have her along," declared Darcy.

"Do you have anyone else you would like to add to the list?" asked Pastor Paul. Darcy and Kyle looked at each other and shook their heads no. "Well, then, we have a team," he said happily. "Oh, by the way, does Mary Anne have a passport?"

"Yes," affirmed Darcy. "She's good to go."

The Ugandans couldn't have been more helpful and accommodating in seeing to it that everyone secured visas in record time. It wasn't long before everyone was cleared for travel and tickets had been purchased. Darcy was pleased that everything was going so smoothly, but not a bit surprised. God's hand was in this. It had been from the beginning.

Ed and Andrea Hardesty kept in touch with the Carseys as much as their undependable computer service allowed. They had graciously offered to meet the work team at the airport, even though it was a considerable distance from them. Darcy and Kyle had accepted the offer gratefully, and had insisted that *Tell Them So* would cover their expenses.

Along with the building materials, tools and supplies, Kyle and Darcy arranged for tents and camping gear to be delivered to the work site. Most of the men on the work team had not camped much, but they all promised they would be as flexible as the job demanded and were more than happy to rough it. Surprisingly, Mary Anne was the most experienced camper among them.

Darcy wrote in her blessing book nightly during the preparation phase of the project. She covered page after page, filling one book and then another, and was now into a third. She never once let it concern her how quickly money was flowing out of the bank. It was flowing in as well. Keeping a healthy balance was in the Lord's hands, and she had no trouble at all casting that care upon Him.

Andrea Hardesty had actually gotten in touch with Jim Baxter and *TELL THEM SO* was now being sold in Uganda. Darcy could hardly wrap her mind around it. She thought back to that day when she had gotten that first call from Jim and he had said that he wanted to publish her book. What a long way they had come, and what an exciting journey it had been! Her dreams were coming true beyond anything she could have ever imagined. But wasn't that just how the Lord worked!

CHAPTER TWENTY-SIX

ON THE DAY THE TEAM was scheduled to depart, Kyle and Darcy drove Mary Anne to the airport. Kyle pulled into a parking spot and the ladies were jumping out of the car before he could turn off the engine. There was practically no luggage. Mary Anne had limited herself to a huge purse and a carry- on bag.

Entering the airport, they found the rest of the team waiting for them so they could all go through security together. Pastor Paul was there as well, and he led the group in a short prayer. Darcy and Kyle stayed long enough to actually watch the jet plane ascend into the air.

It was hard to wait for news from the work team. Kyle had told them not to worry about trying to communicate trans-continentally, but to bring back good reports and lots and lots of pictures. Therefore, he and Darcy were thrilled when they began receiving e-mailed images of the construction. The U.S. team had been joined by the Ugandan workers and progress was being made at an amazing speed. Before Darcy knew it, she and Kyle were on their way back to the airport to pick up Mary Anne and to greet the rest of the team.

The work team, now bonded in Christian love and friendship, bounded off the plane and into the airport. Mary Anne flew into Darcy's arms; they embraced and wept. Kyle was shaking everyone's hands and patting everyone on the back. As the enthusiastic reunion wound down, Kyle suggested that the weary travelers go home and get some rest. He invited everyone to meet at the buffet restaurant the next evening for a full report over a delicious American meal. Everyone cheered.

The team took the buffet by storm. Each of the men had brought their wives and everyone listened attentively to the seemingly inexhaustible supply of stories there were to be shared. Kyle and Darcy were presented with a large file with a full report of the work and the promised plethora of pictures. Tom Lister said that he had given the local populace an A+ on their willingness to be of help, and told Darcy and Kyle that there were not words enough to express their gratitude for the beautiful new school. They could hardly believe that the expenses of operating the school and the children's school fees were all going to be provided.

Mary Anne was bubbling throughout the whole evening. She had earned her keep on the job in a hundred different ways and had still had time to fall in love with the villagers, especially the children. She had left her heart in Africa, and had vowed she'd be going back.

After everyone had eaten all they could possibly eat and told every story they could think of to tell and answered all of Kyle and Darcy's questions, the jet lagged travelers departed, each to their own home, to sleep, and to dream of Africa.

CHAPTER TWENTY-SEVEN

KYLE AND DARCY WATCHED JOYFULLY as their youngest child walked across the platform and receive her nursing degree. It was as exciting a day for them as it was for her. It had been their goal since the day they became parents to see that their children received college educations. They were grateful to God for making that possible, and they were glad that both Jared and Claire had stayed the course.

Over dinner that evening in the fanciest restaurant in the city, Claire entertained her family with stories, some of them confessions, of several of her college experiences. Kyle looked at her occasionally with expressions of mock sternness, but he was actually glad to hear that his daughter, who always took herself so seriously, had allowed herself a little fun while at school. Jared had, goodness knows! If the truth were to be told, Kyle had engaged in more mischief during his own college years than either of his kids had been. Of course, that wasn't anything the kids needed to know.

Jared would be going right back to work the next day, but Claire was coming home. She was going to allow herself a very short vacation with her folks and then buckle down and study for her licensing examination. Knowing Claire, it would be a short rest, indeed. She was an amazingly focused individual.

After laughing over Claire's hilarious account of the morning she had gotten up and discovered that every pair of underwear she owned was missing, and how she had to follow scavenger hunt type clues in order to recover them, Kyle suddenly grew serious.

"Kids, there is something your mother and I need you to do for us," Kyle said.

"Why, sure, Dad, what do you need?" asked Jared.

"We know that you both have passports, but you are going to have to get some visas. We've done the ground work on that and there isn't much left to do but get your signatures. Oh, and sorry, but you'll have to get several shots."

"Shots?" asked Jared, eagerly. "Where we going that we need shots?"

Kyle looked at Darcy and saw the tears swimming in her eyes. She smiled at him and nodded. "We are going to Uganda!" he practically shouted.

"Uganda? As in Africa, Uganda?" squealed Claire as she jumped out of her seat. Several diners glanced her way and smiled. She self-consciously sat back down.

"That's where Uganda is," said Darcy.

"Wow!" said both Jared and Kyle simultaneously.

"How did this come about, Dad? I mean, why Uganda?" asked Jared.

Kyle replied "Kids, you both know how much your Grand wanted to be a missionary and make an impact on the world for the Lord," stated Kyle.

"Sure," said Jared. "Then our grandfather died and she didn't get to go. She became a teacher instead. Only Mom wrote *Tell Them So* and showed how Grand really did make an impact on the world-a bigger one than she ever knew-by being a blessing to one person after another."

"Exactly," said Kyle. He was doing all the talking because he and his wife had agreed beforehand that Darcy would be too emotional to do it without crying.

"Well, here's the deal. Grand didn't get to go to the mission field, but it would mean a lot to your mother and me if we could all go in her place. She was always especially drawn to Africa. Now that there is enough money in the *Tell Them So* account, we want to do just that-go in Grand's place. Since Grand was a teacher and cared so much about education, we want to take some educational material to a school for orphans over there. You want to go, don't you? Are you in?"

Both Jared and his sister shouted "Yes!" They then turned to each other and lifted their right hands. The *HIGH-FIVE* they gave each other made Kyle roll his eyes.

Kyle explained to Jared that he had cleared his calendar for him. He had spoken with Jared's bosses and had requested that he be given time off for this extraordinary experience. When he had tried to give them copies of *Tell Them So*, he had discovered that Jared had already done so and that had already read the book. Under the circumstances, enthusiastic permission had been granted for Hannah's grandson to take time away from his job for such a trip. Jared would get his shots on his own and then come home a couple of days before their flight, which was scheduled for the second week of July. Jared couldn't believe he was getting the time off, but Kyle explained to him that his bosses wanted him to make a video presentation of the experience that would be suitable for a chapel presentation at camp and for their Missionary Youth conventions.

Preparations began almost immediately for overseas travel. Visas were readily secured for Jared and Claire; Kyle and Darcy had theirs already. Darcy had made an appointment for them to get their shots. The women endured theirs bravely; Kyle turned out to be the biggest baby.

Darcy gave Claire and Jared very specific directions for packing. "Now, listen," she told them, "pack as few clothes as possible. I'm going to need room in each bag for the educational materials we're taking. Whatever you do, don't take anything you can't live without. Except for the clothes we will be wearing on the trip home, we are going to leave everything behind for the Ugandans."

The thought of giving her clothes away captured Claire's heart. She tore through her closet, pulling out everything that might be suitable for the climate in Uganda. By the time she was finished, all her bags were stuffed full of clothing. Darcy's heart warmed to see her daughter's generosity, but had to remind her that room was needed in her luggage for the school supplies. Reluctantly, Claire repacked her bags, but having already committed to giving away the clothing, she set the items aside for the homeless shelter.

Packing was no problem for Jared- enough underwear, no socks, three pairs of khaki shorts and five tee-shirts. Done!

Kyle had the easiest packing job of all as he left it all up to Darcy. She had been busy doing research on exactly what would and would not be allowed on the plane. She unpacked and repacked each piece of luggage until everything met with her own personal inspection. As she had eliminated every item that could possibly be impermissible, she felt confident that the inspection at the airport would go well.

The day finally came when the Carsey family was ready to leave for Uganda.

Every item on every check list had been checked off. Then every list had been rechecked. The family was ready to fly to Africa.

"Now listen, everyone," said Darcy. "You have to wear real shoes on the plane. No flip-flops or sandals."

"Why, Mom? Isn't that exactly what we'll be wearing in Uganda?" asked Claire.

"Yes," answered Darcy, "but this is what I read recently. Shoes that aren't securely attached to your feet can fly off in the event of a plane crash and be impossible to find. Then you have to walk barefooted over broken glass, twisted metal, and maybe even through fire, to get out of the plane."

"Oh, Mom," protested Jared in that tone that every parent has heard at one time or another.

"I have spoken. Wear your sensible shoes on the plane. Wear your flip-flops or sandals in Africa. Wear your sensible shoes on the plane when we come home."

Jared started to respond, but Kyle sent him an unspoken *LISTEN TO YOUR MOTHER* communication. Jared shrugged and said "All righty, then".

"Other than having to pay extra fees for overweight luggage, which Darcy had fully anticipated, the Carseys successfully navigated the airport. They found themselves headed for Detroit right on schedule. Once they arrived there, they settled in for a long layover. Darcy was pleasantly surprised to meet a couple who had read her book. They listened with interest as she and Kyle filled them in on everything that had happened since the book had been published. Jared and Claire had gone off to explore the airport and to buy snacks for the trans-Atlantic flight. Their parents didn't see them again until shortly before they were supposed to board the jumbo jet.

There were so many things Darcy wanted to remember about the trip, but the one thing that she knew would be truly unforgettable was the thrill she felt when she got her first glimpse of Africa. It didn't seem real. She could hardly believe she would soon set foot on African soil. When the announcement came over the loudspeaker for the passengers to prepare for landing, Darcy squeezed Kyle's hand tightly. He looked at her and saw on her face an expression that revealed her mixed emotions.

"What are you thinking, honey?" asked Kyle, even though he was certain that he knew.

"I'm thinking about my mother," Darcy answered softly. "I'm so happy to be here and yet sad that she never got to be here herself."

Kyle patted Darcy's knee. "God works in mysterious ways, my dear, and sometimes in miraculous ones. He's made her dreams come true, but He used you to make that happen. Why things happen the way they do is sometimes something that only He in His wisdom can know."

The plane began its descent and Darcy turned a little pale as she closed her eyes and gripped the arm of her seat. Kyle, who had always been comfortable with flying, couldn't quit grinning as he felt himself safely delivered to terra firma- *AFRICAN* terra firma.

Soon, everyone was gathering up all their belongings and carry-on luggage. Jared and Claire connected with their parents and the family made their way to the front of the plane. Jared smirked and commented that it was sure a good thing that they had all worn their sensible shoes. Claire laughed out loud and gave her brother a gentle shove. Kyle wisely made no comment.

It was hot when they disembarked-stifling hot. Darcy thought to herself that this was even hotter than she had expected. Kyle muttered under his breath, "My goodness, it is hot," but very softly as he did not want to be the first one to complain. They made their way across the tarmac and into a building where conditions were even more sweltering, given the crowd of people and the absence of windows.

Standing in line with their passports in hand, they took in the sights and sounds and smells of their first exposure to the continent of Africa. Everything was exciting to them. Listening to languages they had never heard before, they were fascinated by the beautiful accents of the speakers. Darcy and Claire were especially interested in the gorgeous, colorful outfits worn by the women-and the men as well. There were many men dressed in apparel that was vastly different from the clothes worn by American men. The ladies could see already that they were going to thoroughly enjoy this exposure to another culture.

As soon as the Carseys had been granted official permission to enter the country, Kyle began looking about expectantly. Off to the right, next to the baggage retrieval conveyor, there stood a young couple smiling and waving. Kyle nudged Darcy, who looked up and began waving enthusiastically in return. They hurried over to the pleasant young man and woman, who were white of skin, but dressed in bright African garb. The tall, brown haired man wore a green and gold tunic type cotton shirt over khaki pants. On his feet were sandals that had been well broken in a long time ago. The petite young red head at his side was clad in a light cotton dress made of beautiful purple, orange and yellow fabric. Jared and Claire, trailing behind their parents, wondered who these people could be.

Extending his right hand to Kyle, Ed Hardesty spoke first. "You're the Carseys! I'm Ed and this is my wife Andrea. Welcome to Uganda!"

Darcy and Andrea were already embracing each other affectionately. Darcy then hugged Ed as she would an old family friend. Beckoning to Jared and Claire, she said, "Kids, meet Ed and Andrea Hardesty. They are missionaries here in Uganda. We've been in touch with them over the internet and they are going to take us to the school where we are donating the educational materials. Ed, Andrea, this is our son, Jared, and our daughter, Claire."

"It's wonderful to finally meet you," said Andrea Hardesty. We've heard so much about you."

"Thank you," responded Jared. "It sure is nice to have someone here to greet us."

"How long have you been in Uganda?" asked Claire. Ed Hardesty told her that they had first come to the country nearly five years ago. He described briefly the work he and Andrea were doing there. He then suggested that they get everyone's luggage gathered up, after which he would drive them to their hotel.

After navigating through the building and across the parking lot, the family piled into a battered white van. It appeared to be freshly washed, but not much could be done about the dings and dents and scratches. A couple of hefty young men threw their baggage unto the roof of the van and secured it all with rope. Ed tipped the fellows and thanked them. Kyle would have liked to take care of it, but had not yet exchanged any currency.

Once Darcy, Kyle and their children were checked into the motel and shown to clean, comfortable rooms, the Hardesty's excused themselves and retreated to their own quarters. "Get some rest," they said in parting. "Tomorrow is going to be a big day!" It was such a treat for Ed and Andrea to be staying at the nice hotel; it was a bit of a vacation for them. Kyle and Darcy were handling the expenses.

Darcy had been certain she would not be able to sleep a wink. How could she? She crawled into bed, stretched out her travel weary body, and the next thing she knew Kyle was gently shaking her foot and saying "Wake up, sleepyhead!" She forced open her eyes and there stood Kyle with wet hair; a large white towel was wrapped around his mid-section.

"You'd better get moving, lady. We have a busy day ahead of us."

Darcy jumped out of bed and headed for the bathroom. She called out to Kyle that he ought to wake Jared and Claire. Just then there was a knock on the door. Jared hollered, "Hey you guys- are you ready for breakfast? I'm starving!"

As soon as everyone had finished a hearty and, in Jared's words, practically normal breakfast they all hurried to once again climb into the old white van.

"I am sorry the roads here are not like what you are used to in the States," apologized Ed as he pulled out of the hotel parking lot.

"Oh, I was thinking they were really pretty good," commented Kyle. Ed and Andrea both laughed.

"What?" asked Jared.

"You'll see," was all that Ed would say.

Presently, the van traveled beyond the city limits and the road became a little bumpier. Before long, the passengers were being thrown about as the van bounced in and out of ruts almost as big as the vehicle itself. The road was horrendous, but the scenery made up for it. Ed and Andrea enjoyed their role as tour guides and pointed out all kinds of things of interest along the way. They could hardly go a mile without one Carsey or another crying out "Look at that!"

After four and a half long, steamy hours of trying to sip bottled water between bumps, the dust-caked van slowed as it approached a village. As Ed applied the vehicle's brakes, children came running toward them, cheering and laughing. "Everybody out," instructed Ed.

Darcy stepped out of the van first, carrying a small tote made in a pink tulip covered print fabric. Claire joined her mother and two adorable little bald girls instantly approached. The children each took one of Claire's hands and beamed up at her. Andrea patted the girls on their heads and said something in Lugandan that made both children laugh.

Once all six travelers had emerged from the van, they were approached by a thin young girl with a pronounced limp. "Carsey family, we welcome you to Uganda. Thank you for coming. God bless you," she said, shyly, and in heavily accented English. The child spoke formally and Darcy realized that this young lady had been given the honor of being their official greeter. She stepped forward and gave the girl a tender hug.

"This way, please," motioned Ed Hardesty. He began walking and the rest of the party fell in behind him. Darcy wanted to walk hand-in-hand with her children, but the pathway was too narrow. The group proceeded, single file, with Ed and Andrea leading the way. Darcy followed closely behind Andrea. Jared came next, and then Clair; Kyle brought up the rear.

Passing a grove of mango trees, the path curved to the left. Rounding the curve, the landscape opened up and the party entered a clearing. There appeared before them an attractive, brand new building and a well equipped playground. Across the front of the building, in large, neat letters were the words HANNAH M. MILLER MEMORIAL ELEMENTARY SCHOOL. Jared and Claire stopped in their tracks. Claire began to cry.

As Darcy reached into her tote for her mother's ashes, Jared, overwhelmed, asked "Mom, did you build this school?"

With tears streaming down her cheeks, Darcy put her arms around her children. "Your Grand built this school," she told them. "Grand and God built it."

THE END

ABOUT THE AUTHOR

IT WAS THROUGH THE EXPERIENCE of surviving cancer that Jackie Baters found the inspiration for this novel, her first book. She and her husband Dennis are thankful that their daughter and son-in-law have given them three beautiful grandchildren; of all the things Jackie is grateful she has lived to see, those three little faces are at the top of the list. She and Dennis live in southeastern Oklahoma.